without the | pasta
the | and rice
calories | Justine Pattison

Low-calorie recipes, cheats and ideas for guilt-free carbs

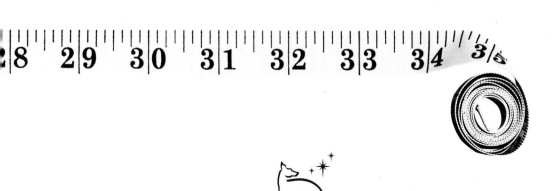

contents

introduction

MY STORY

I struggled with my weight for years. After being a skinny child and teenager, I piled on the weight during my last years of school and went into my twenties feeling fat and frumpy. A career as a cookery writer and food stylist has helped me understand good food but because my kitchen is always overflowing with great things to eat, temptation is never far away. My weight yo-yoed for twenty years and at my heaviest I weighed more than 15 stone.

A few years ago, I worked on the hit TV series *You Are What You Eat* – I put together those groaning tables of bad food. I also had the chance to work with the contributors on the show, guiding them through the dieting process and helping them discover a whole new way of eating and cooking. Having been overweight myself, I became passionate about helping people lose weight.

Since then, I've worked as a food consultant on many of the weight-loss shows you've seen on TV, and written diet plans and recipes for best-selling books, newspapers and magazines. I'm thrilled that thousands of people have successfully followed my way of cooking and lost weight.

This book, and the others in the *Without the Calories* series, are ideal for anyone who wants to lose weight while leading a normal life. Cooking my way will help you sustain a happy, healthy weight loss. That's what it's all about: you don't have to be stick thin, but you deserve to feel good about yourself. My *Without the Calories* recipes will help you reach your goal.

ABOUT THIS BOOK

Very few things are as comforting as a large bowl of freshly cooked pasta or steaming hot risotto, but dishes high in starchy carbohydrates, perhaps teamed with a creamy sauce, can be hideously high in calories and are the last thing you need when you are trying to lose weight.

In this book, I've taken classic pasta and rice dishes and given them a healthy makeover. I've reworked the ingredients to reduce the number of calories as much as possible, while still keeping the flavour and appeal of the original. You'll find that these new recipes have been rebalanced to contain more fibre-rich vegetables, lean protein and less fat. You can add even more fibre by using wholemeal pasta and brown rice rather than white, but you'll need to adjust the cooking times accordingly.

I'm not going to make rash promises about how many pounds you will shed, but I do know that when it comes to losing weight, finding foods that give you pleasure and fit into your lifestyle are the key to success. When you eat well without obsessing over rapid weight loss, it's easier to relax and lose what you need to comfortably – and safely.

To help everyone enjoy these reinvented dishes, I've used easy-to-find ingredients and given clear, simple cooking instructions. There's also freezer information included where appropriate, so you know which dishes you can store safely for another day.

If you're already following a diet plan, you'll find additional nutritional information at the back of the book that'll help you work my recipes into your week. And, if you're stuck for inspiration and have a few pounds to lose, try my 123 Plan. It couldn't be easier.

USING THE 123 PLAN

If you're not following a diet regime at the moment and want a great kick-start, try my 123 Plan for a few weeks. I've tried to make it really easy, and you don't need to do too much adding up. You'll find nearly 500 recipes to choose from in the *Without the Calories* series. Just pick one breakfast or main meal recipe a day from each section to bring your daily intake to between 900 and 1,200 calories. Add an *essential extra* 300 calories a day from a choice of accompaniments, snacks or desserts, and you'll be on your way to a healthy, sustainable weight loss of between 2–3lbs a week.

ONE
up to 300 calories

TWO
300–400 calories

THREE
400–500 calories

YOUR ESSENTIAL EXTRAS

These extra 300 calories can be made up of accompaniments, such as potatoes, rice and pasta, as well as snacks or treats; there are suggestions and serving sizes on page 180. You'll also find recipes that contain under 200 calories a portion, which can be included as part of your essential extras. As long as your extras don't exceed 300 calories a day, you'll be on track.

WHEN TO EAT

The 123 Plan is flexible, so if you find you fancy a **ONE** or **TWO** recipe rather than a **THREE** as your third meal of the day, just add enough calories to bring it into the right range. Don't worry if the calculations aren't absolutely accurate – a difference of 25 or less calories per serving won't affect your weekly allowance.

If you want to add your own favourite meals into the plan, just make sure they are within the recommended calorie boundaries and calculate accordingly. (You may find this useful when planning breakfast especially.)

DON'T RUSH IT

Weight tends to be gained over time, and losing it gradually will make the process easier and help give your body, especially your skin, time to adapt. You're more likely to get into positive, enjoyable long-term cooking and eating habits this way too.

WHAT IS A CALORIE?

Put simply, a calorie is a unit of energy contained within food and drink which our bodies burn as fuel. Different foods contain varying amounts of calories and if more calories are consumed than the body needs, the excess will be stored as fat. To lose weight, we need to eat less or use more energy by increasing our activity – and ideally both!

I've provided the calorie content of a single serving of each dish. In my experience, most people will lose at least 2lb a week by consuming around 1,200–1,500 calories a day, but it's always best to check with your GP before you start a new regime. Everyone is different and, especially if you have several stones to lose, you'll need some personalised advice. The calories contained in each recipe have been calculated as accurately as possible, but could vary a little depending on your ingredients. If you have a couple of days of eating more than 1,400 calories, try to eat closer to 1,100 for the next few days. Over a week, things will even out.

My recipes strike a balance between eating and cooking well and reducing calories, and I've tried them all as part of my own way of enjoying food without putting on excess weight. Even if you don't need to lose weight, I hope you enjoy cooking from my books simply because you like the recipes.

SECRETS OF SUCCESS

The serving sizes that I've recommended form the basis of the nutritional information on page 182, and if you eat any more, you may find losing weight takes longer. If you're cooking for anyone who doesn't need to watch their calorie intake, you can increase their servings, but bear in mind that too much sugar isn't good for anyone.

The right portion size also holds the key to maintaining your weight loss. Use this opportunity to get used to smaller servings. Work out exactly how much food your body needs to maintain the shape that makes you feel great. That way, even when counting calories feels like a distant memory, you'll remain in control of your eating habits.

Stick to lean protein (which will help you feel fuller for longer) and vegetables and avoid high-fat, high-sugar snacks and confectionery. Be aware that alcohol is packed with empty calories and could weaken your resolve. Starchy carbs such as pasta, rice, potatoes and bread are kept to a minimum because I've found that, combined with eating lots of veg and good protein, this leads to more sustainable weight loss. There's no need to avoid dairy products such as cheese and cream, although they tend to be high in fat and calories. You can swap the high-fat versions for reduced-fat ones, or use less.

Ditch heavily processed foods and you will feel so much better. Switching to more natural ingredients will help your body work with you.

Most recipes in the *Without the Calories* series form the main part of each meal, so there's room to have your plate half-filled with freshly cooked vegetables or a colourful, crunchy salad. This will help fill you up, and boost your intake of vitamins and minerals.

Make sure you drink enough fluids, especially water – around 2 litres is ideal. Staying hydrated will help you lose weight more comfortably, and it's important when you exercise too.

IN THE KITCHEN

Pick up some electronic kitchen scales and a set of measuring spoons if you don't already have them. Both will probably cost less than a takeaway meal for two, and will help ensure good results.

Invest, if you can, in a large, deep non-stick frying pan, a medium non-stick saucepan and a large saucepan for pasta (so it can bubble freely in the pot). The non-stick coating means that you will need less oil to cook, and a frying pan with a wide base and deep sides can double as a wok. Non-stick baking parchment will prevent sticking and means you can use less oil. Look at the oven temperatures carefully.

I use oil and butter sparingly, and use a natural spray oil for frying. I also keep a jam jar containing a little sunflower oil and a heatproof pastry brush to hand for greasing pans lightly before baking and frying.

STICK WITH IT

Shifting your eating habits and trying to lose weight is not easy, especially if you have been eating the same way for many years. But it isn't too late. You may never have the perfect body, but you can have one that, fuelled by really good food, makes you feel happy and healthy. For more information, tips and ideas, visit www.justinepattison.co.uk.

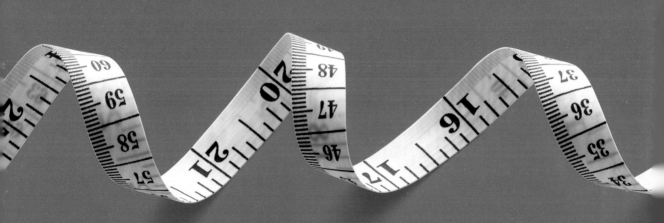

quick
dishes

151 CALORIES PER SERVING

summer minestrone

SERVES 4

PREP: 15 MINUTES

COOK: 20 MINUTES

2 tsp olive oil
1 medium onion, finely
    chopped
2 garlic cloves, thinly sliced
2 medium carrots, peeled
    and cut into roughly
    1.5cm chunks
4 large ripe tomatoes, diced
1.5 litres chicken stock
    (made with 1½ stock
    cubes)
50g tiny pasta shells or
    dried spaghetti, broken
    into short lengths
2 tbsp tomato purée
2 medium courgettes, cut
    into roughly 1.5cm chunks
100g fresh or frozen peas
100g fine green beans,
    cut into roughly 2cm
    lengths
flaked sea salt
ground black pepper

Flat freeze the cooked and
cooled soup in freezer bags
for up to 3 months. Rinse
the bags under hot water
for a few seconds then
break the frozen soup into
a wide-based, non-stick
saucepan. Add a splash of
water and reheat, stirring
regularly until piping hot
throughout.

A light and fresh-tasting soup, packed with vegetables in a fresh tomato broth. The pasta makes it extra filling, so there is no need to serve it with bread.

Heat the oil in a large non-stick saucepan and fry the onion gently for 5 minutes or until softened but not coloured, stirring often. Add the garlic and carrots to the pan with the onion. Stir over a low heat for about 1 minute.

Stir in the diced tomatoes, pour over the chicken stock, add the tomato purée and bring to the boil. Drop the pasta gently into the pan. Cook for 8 minutes, stirring occasionally.

Reduce the heat slightly, add the courgettes, peas and green beans and simmer for a further 5 minutes more, or until the pasta is just tender.

Season the soup with salt and lots of black pepper. Serve in warm, deep bowls, topped with pesto sauce or Parmesan if you like, but don't forget to add the extra calories.

374

creamy chicken and parmesan fettuccine

SERVES 4

PREP: 10 MINUTES

COOK: 12 MINUTES

200g dried fettuccine or
  tagliatelle
oil, for brushing or spraying
2 boneless, skinless chicken
  breasts (each about 175g),
  cut into roughly 2.5cm
  chunks
15g butter
20g plain flour
300ml semi-skimmed milk
25g Parmesan, finely grated
15g bunch of fresh curly or
  flat-leaf parsley, leaves
  finely chopped
flaked sea salt
ground black pepper

Tip: Use a silicone-covered
whisk to break up any
lumps in your sauce but
don't worry if it isn't
perfectly smooth, as it
won't show once the
pasta is mixed through.

A luxurious tasting chicken and pasta dish. The sauce tastes
deliciously rich and creamy, but the combination of semi-
skimmed milk with minimal amounts of butter and Parmesan
is deceptive. Serve with lots of freshly cooked vegetables
or a salad.

Half fill a large saucepan with water and bring it to the boil.
Tip the pasta into the boiling water and cook for 8–10 minutes,
or according to the packet instructions, until tender, stirring
occasionally.

While the pasta is cooking, brush or spray a large non-stick
frying pan with oil and place over a high heat. Add the chicken,
season well with salt and pepper and stir-fry for 3–4 minutes
until lightly coloured. Tip onto a plate and return the pan to
the heat.

Add the butter and as soon as it has melted, reduce the heat
to medium and stir in the flour and cook for a few seconds.
Gradually add the milk, stirring continuously until it is all
combined and then bring to a gentle simmer.

Stir in the chicken and the Parmesan. Simmer gently for
3–4 minutes, or until the chicken is thoroughly cooked,
stirring regularly. Adjust the seasoning to taste.

Drain the pasta in a colander and return to the saucepan.
Add the creamy chicken, Parmesan sauce and the parsley
and toss together well.

403
CALORIES
PER SERVING

easy green chicken curry with spinach rice

SERVES 4

PREP: 15 MINUTES

COOK: 20 MINUTES

6 boneless, skinless chicken thighs (about 500g)

3 tbsp Thai green curry paste (from a jar)

1 tbsp Thai fish sauce (nam pla)

4 tsp cornflour

400ml can reduced-fat coconut milk

6 kaffir lime leaves, fresh, frozen or dried

15g bunch fresh coriander, leaves finely chopped

175g baby corn, trimmed and halved

1 red pepper, deseeded and cut into roughly 2.5cm chunks

1 yellow or orange pepper, deseeded and cut into roughly 2.5cm chunks

FOR THE RICE

150g basmati or Thai jasmine rice

100g young spinach leaves

2 spring onions, trimmed and thinly sliced (optional)

Tip: Any leftover fresh kaffir lime leaves can be frozen in a zip-seal bag for several months. I always keep a bag in my freezer and use them from frozen to add extra flavour to Thai-style curries.

Kaffir lime leaves make this curry taste particularly delicious and authentic and help to balance the flavour of a ready-made curry paste. You can find fresh leaves in the veg aisle of larger supermarkets; otherwise frozen or dried leaves will do.

Trim any visible fat off the chicken thighs – a set of kitchen scissors work well – and cut each into 3 pieces.

Put the curry paste in a large non-stick frying pan, add the chicken and cook over a medium heat for 3 minutes, stirring until the chicken is lightly coloured on all sides. Mix the fish sauce with the cornflour until smooth.

Pour the coconut milk into the pan and stir in the fish sauce and cornflour, lime leaves, coriander and all the vegetables. Bring to a gentle simmer and cook for 15 minutes or until the chicken is tender, stirring occasionally.

While the chicken is cooking, half fill a medium pan with water and bring it to the boil. Add the rice, stir and return to the boil. Cook for about 10 minutes, or according to the packet instructions, until tender. Add the spinach leaves and spring onions, if using, and cook for 1 minute more, stirring. Drain the rice in a colander and fluff up with a fork. Serve with the curry. (Don't eat the lime leaves.)

369

CALORIES
PER SERVING

stir-fried orange beef with spring onion rice

SERVES 3

PREP: 15 MINUTES

COOK: 15 MINUTES

2 medium oranges
20g chunk of fresh
    root ginger
350g thin-cut beef frying
    steak, trimmed of hard
    fat and cut into thin strips
1 tsp ground ginger
1 tbsp cornflour
2 tbsp dark soy sauce
1 tbsp sunflower oil
1 red pepper, deseeded
    and thinly sliced
1 green pepper, deseeded
    and thinly sliced
2 garlic cloves, very
    thinly sliced
250g sachet of ready-
    cooked basmati rice
6 spring onions, trimmed
    and thinly sliced
flaked sea salt
ground black pepper

Tip: If you want to cook fresh rice instead of using the ready-cooked kind for this dish, boil 125g rinsed basmati rice in a pan of water for about 8 minutes or until just tender, stirring occasionally. Add the sliced spring onions and cook for 1 minute more. Drain well.

A zingy stir-fry made with thin frying steak, which is usually very lean and cheaper than many other cuts. If you can't find it in your local supermarket, choose lean rump or sirloin steak instead.

Peel the rind from a quarter of one of the oranges with a potato peeler and place on a board. Cut the rind into very thin matchsticks, roughly 5cm long and 2mm wide.

Put the rind matchsticks in a heatproof bowl, cover with just-boiled water and set aside (this will help them soften). Peel the ginger and cut it into similar sized matchsticks. Cut the oranges in half and squeeze the juice. You need 150ml of orange juice (you may need to add a little water if necessary).

Put the beef in a bowl and toss it with the ginger, a good pinch of salt and lots of ground black pepper. Mix the cornflour with 2 tablespoons of the orange juice in a separate bowl until smooth, then stir in the soy sauce and remaining orange juice and put the sauce to one side.

Heat 1 teaspoon of the oil in a large non-stick frying pan or wok over a high heat and stir-fry the beef in 2 batches until well browned, adding a teaspoon more oil between batches. Each batch will take 2–3 minutes. Once each batch is cooked put it to one side on a plate.

Drain the orange rind in a sieve. Return the frying pan to the heat, add the remaining oil and stir-fry the peppers for 2 minutes, then add the garlic, ginger and orange rind and cook for 1 minute more. Add a splash of water if they begin to stick.

Return the meat to the pan, pour over the reserved sauce and stir-fry together for 2 minutes or until the beef is hot and glossy. While the beef is cooking, toss the rice with the sliced spring onions and reheat according to the packet instructions until piping hot throughout.

458

italian marsala pork with spinach rice

500g pork tenderloin (fillet)
2 tbsp sunflower oil
200g easy-cook, long grain rice
250g chestnut mushrooms, thickly sliced
2 medium onions, thinly sliced
2 tbsp plain flour
2 tsp paprika (not smoked)
300ml beef or pork stock (made with 1 stock cube)
3 tbsp Marsala or Madeira wine
3 tbsp half-fat crème fraiche or soured cream
100g young spinach leaves
flaked sea salt
ground black pepper
freshly chopped parsley (optional)

Flat freeze the cooked and cooled pork and sauce in a freezer bag for up to 3 months. Thaw overnight in the fridge and reheat with 200ml of water in a frying pan for about 20 minutes, or microwave, stirring occasionally until piping hot throughout.

Tip: You can save time by pouring just-boiled water from a kettle into the saucepan for cooking the rice and returning it to the boil.

Marsala is a sweet Italian wine that can be used for desserts and savoury dishes. It goes particularly well with pork and mushrooms, as this quick supper dish proves.

Trim the pork of any fat and sinew and slice on a slight diagonal into discs about 5mm thick. Season well with salt and lots of freshly ground black pepper.

Heat 1 tablespoon of oil in a large non-stick frying pan or wok and fry the pork in 3 batches over a high heat for 1–2 minutes until nicely browned on each side but not cooked through. Transfer to a plate. Make sure the pork is well browned as this adds real depth of flavour to the final dish.

While the pork is cooking, half fill a large saucepan with water and bring it to the boil. Add the rice, stir well and return to the boil. Cook for about 10 minutes or until tender, stirring regularly. Add the spinach in the last minute of cooking time.

Add the rest of the oil, the mushrooms and onions to the frying pan and cook for 4–5 minutes or until the onions are softened and the mushrooms are well browned.

Stir in the flour and paprika then gradually add the stock and Marsala or Madeira. Bring to the boil, stirring continuously. Reduce the heat slightly and simmer for 2 minutes, stirring.

Add the crème fraiche or soured cream, then return the pork to the pan and cook for a few seconds more until hot, stirring continuously. Drain the rice in a colander, divide between 4 plates and serve with the pork. Garnish with freshly chopped parsley, if you like.

503

CALORIES
PER SERVING

spicy sausage pasta

SERVES 4

PREP: 15 MINUTES

COOK: 30 MINUTES

400g spicy pork sausages
(such as chilli pork)
75g diced smoked lardons
(or smoked streaky
bacon, diced)
1 medium onion, finely
chopped
3 large ripe tomatoes
200g dried pasta shapes,
such as fusilli or penne
75ml red wine
2 tbsp tomato purée
handful of fresh basil,
roughly torn (optional)

A full favoured simple supper dish that uses smoked bacon and sausages to make a rich, tasty sauce for pasta. It's higher in fat than some of my other dishes but is packed with punchy flavours, so a little goes a long way. Use pork sausages flavoured with extra chilli or spices, or add half a teaspoon of dried chilli flakes to the sauce. Serve with a large, lightly dressed mixed salad.

Snip between each sausage to separate and squeeze the meat out of the skins. Place a large non-stick frying pan over a medium heat. Add the lardons, sausage meat and onion. Cook together for about 20 minutes, until well browned, stirring regularly to break up the sausage meat. You want it to become quite sticky and to pick up lots of smoky flavours.

While the onion and sausage meat are cooking, half fill a large saucepan with water and bring it to the boil. Make a small cross in the bottom of each tomato and add them to the water. Dunk for about 30 seconds and then remove them with a slotted spoon and put them on a chopping board to cool for a short while. Add the pasta to the same water and return it to the boil. Cook for 10–12 minutes, or according to the packet instructions, until tender.

When the tomatoes are cool enough to handle, slip off the skins and roughly chop the flesh, discarding the tough central cores. Pour the wine into the frying pan and add the tomatoes and tomato purée. Cook for a further 5–9 minutes or until rich and thick, stirring regularly.

Drain the cooked pasta and return it to the saucepan. Tip the sausage mixture into the same pan and toss well together. Spoon into warmed bowls and serve scattered with torn basil leaves if you like.

329
CALORIES
PER SERVING

pea and prosciutto pasta

SERVES 4

PREP: 5 MINUTES

COOK: 12 MINUTES

200g dried pasta shapes,
  such as gigli or penne
15g butter
1 small onion, thinly sliced
1 garlic clove, crushed
6 slices of prosciutto, torn
  into wide strips
100ml single cream
150g frozen peas
ground black pepper

Tip: You can cut the calories
further by brushing the pan
with a little oil rather than
frying the onion in butter
and reducing the single
cream to 50ml. This will
save about 49 calories
per serving.

A simple, creamy pasta dish that's a doddle to knock together.
Prosciutto is cheaper than Parma ham as it comes from other
areas of Italy, but you can use Serrano ham or even smoked
British ham if you like.

Half fill a large pan with water and bring it to the boil. Add the
pasta and cook for 10–12 minutes, or according to the packet
instructions, until tender.

While the pasta is cooking, melt the butter in a medium
non-stick frying pan and gently cook the onion for 3 minutes
or until very tender, stirring regularly. If the onion starts to
stick, just add a splash of water and continue cooking. Stir in
the garlic and prosciutto and cook for a few seconds more.

Stir in the single cream and the peas. Season with black pepper
and warm together gently for 1–2 minutes, stirring regularly.
Don't let the sauce simmer or the cream may separate.

Drain the pasta and return it to the saucepan. Tip the sauce on
top and toss together with 2 forks until combined. Divide the
pasta between 4 warmed plates and serve with a large salad.

315
CALORIES
PER SERVING

broccoli, tuna and lemon chilli spaghetti

SERVES 2

PREP: 5 MINUTES

COOK: 12 MINUTES

150g long-stemmed
   broccoli
100g dried spaghetti
100g cherry tomatoes,
   halved
1 tbsp olive oil
¼–½ tsp dried chilli flakes
   (depending on taste)
2 tbsp fresh lemon juice
120g can tuna steak, in
   water or brine, drained
flaked sea salt
ground black pepper

Tip: Any long pasta shape,
such as tagliatelle or
linguine, will work just as
well as the spaghetti. And
even short pasta shapes
can be substituted – simply
adjust the cooking times
accordingly.

**A really easy supper for two, this colourful pasta dish is filling
and very delicious. Add chilli to suit your own taste – I always
plump for half a teaspoon but you may prefer to tread a bit
more carefully the first time you try it.**

Half fill a large saucepan with water and bring it to the boil.
Trim the broccoli and cut each stem into 3 pieces, leaving the
heads whole.

Add the spaghetti to the boiling water, return to the boil and
cook for 9 minutes, stirring occasionally. Add the broccoli to
the pan and cook for 2 minutes more.

Drain the pasta and broccoli in a colander. Then return them
to the pan and add the tomatoes, olive oil, chilli flakes and
lemon juice. Season with salt and pepper.

Cook for 2 minutes, tossing with 2 wooden spoons until the
spaghetti is lightly coated with the spices and the tomatoes
are softened but still holding their shape.

Flake the tuna into the pan and heat with the pasta for 1 minute
more, tossing very gently so it doesn't break up too much. Divide
the pasta between 2 warmed plates using tongs or forks.

473
CALORIES
PER SERVING

hoisin salmon with spring onion rice

SERVES 4

PREP: 5 MINUTES

COOK: 12–15 MINUTES

4 x 140g salmon fillets
oil, for greasing
3 tbsp hoisin sauce (from a jar or bottle)
flaked sea salt
ground black pepper

FOR THE RICE
oil, for brushing or spraying
6 spring onions, trimmed and sliced
500ml cold water
½ chicken or vegetable stock cube
200g easy-cook, long grain rice
15g bunch of fresh coriander, leaves finely chopped, plus a few sprigs to garnish (optional)
ground black pepper
lime wedges, for squeezing

Everyone seems to love this simple salmon dish. Use ready-made hoisin sauce to glaze the salmon as it cooks and serve with fluffy spring onion rice. Even if you are serving fewer than four, it's well worth making the whole recipe as the salmon is also fantastic served cold with salad for lunch the next day.

Preheat the oven to 220°C/Fan 200°C/Gas 7. Place the salmon fillets skin-side down about 5cm apart in a lightly oiled small ovenproof dish and season well. Brush generously with the hoisin sauce. Bake for 12–15 minutes or until just cooked. When the fish is ready, it should look opaque almost all the way through to the centre and begin to flake into large pieces when prodded with a knife.

While the fish is cooking, prepare the rice. Brush or spray a medium saucepan with oil and place over a medium heat. Add the spring onions and cook for 30 seconds, stirring.

Add the water, crumble over the stock cube and bring to the boil. Stir in the rice and cook for 10 minutes, or according to the packet instructions, until the rice is just tender and the stock has been absorbed, stirring occasionally. Add a little extra water if necessary.

Add the chopped coriander (if using), season with ground black pepper and toss well together. Divide the rice between 4 warmed plates. Place the salmon on top and garnish with more coriander. Serve with lime wedges for squeezing.

446
CALORIES
PER SERVING

tagliatelle with smoked salmon

SERVES 2

PREP: 5–8 MINUTES

COOK: 10 MINUTES

150g dried egg tagliatelle
15g butter
1 slender leek, trimmed
   and thinly sliced
75ml single cream
50g sliced smoked salmon,
   cut into long strips
ground black pepper

Only five ingredients are needed to make this super-quick supper for two. I've used single cream rather than double to keep the calories down and added sliced leek for colour and to help stretch the serving to fill you up.

Half fill a large pan with water and bring it to the boil. Add the tagliatelle and cook it for 6–8 minutes, or according to the packet instructions, until tender.

While the pasta is cooking, melt the butter in a large non-stick frying pan and gently cook the leek for 5 minutes or until very tender, stirring regularly. If the leek starts to stick, just add a splash of water and continue cooking.

When the leek is soft, add the single cream and salmon to the pan. Season with black pepper and warm together gently for 1–2 minutes, stirring regularly. Don't let the sauce simmer or the cream may separate.

Drain the pasta and return it to the saucepan. Tip the creamy leek and salmon mixture on top and toss together with 2 forks until combined. Divide the pasta between 2 warmed plates and serve with a large salad.

406

CALORIES
PER SERVING

spaghetti omelette

10g butter
1 tsp sunflower oil
4 spring onions, trimmed
and sliced
4 large eggs
150g cold cooked spaghetti
or other long pasta
150g cherry tomatoes,
halved or quartered
if large
25g mature Cheddar
cheese, coarsely grated
flaked sea salt
ground black pepper

Tip: If you don't have any leftover spaghetti, you can cook some just to serve in this omelette. You should find that 65g of dried spaghetti will give you 150g of cooked spaghetti.

I was thinking along the lines of a Spanish omelette when I came up with the idea for my spaghetti omelette. It's a great way to use up leftover spaghetti and is filling enough to serve without bread. You'll need a frying pan with a metal handle as you finish cooking it under the grill.

Melt the butter with the oil in a medium non-stick flame proof frying pan. The base should have a diameter of about 19cm. Cook the spring onions for 2 minutes or until they are beginning to soften, stirring regularly.

While the onions are softening, beat the eggs in a large bowl with a metal whisk. Season with a pinch of salt and lots of ground black pepper. Stir in the spaghetti and toss with a couple of forks until well mixed.

Pour the egg mixture into the pan. As the eggs begin to set, use a wooden spoon to draw the cooked egg towards the centre 6–7 times, working your way around the pan so the raw egg runs into the spaces left by the cooked egg. Scatter the tomatoes on top.

Cook for about 3 minutes or until the egg is set on the bottom, sprinkle with cheese and then place the pan under a preheated hot grill and cook for 2–3 minutes, or until firm. Carefully loosen the sides with a heatproof palette knife and slide the omelette onto a plate or board, folding it as you go. Divide the omelette between 2 plates and serve with a large mixed salad.

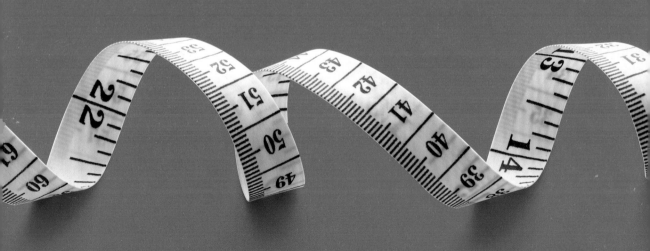

family
favourites

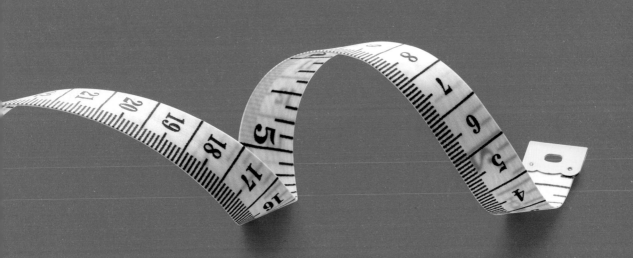

310
CALORIES
PER SERVING

creamy chicken and vegetable pasta

SERVES 4
PREP: 10 MINUTES
COOK: 12 MINUTES

175g dried pasta shapes, such as penne, fusilli or rigatoni
3 rashers smoked back bacon
oil, for brushing or spraying
100g button mushrooms, thickly sliced
2 cooked skinless chicken breasts (each about 100g)
150g cherry tomatoes, halved
150g long-stemmed broccoli, trimmed and each stem cut into three pieces
4 tbsp single cream
flaked sea salt
freshly ground black pepper

Tip: If you don't want to buy cooked chicken breasts, use leftover chicken from a roast or cook a couple of boneless, skinless chicken breasts instead. Simply put the chicken breasts in a small, lightly oiled roasting tin, season with salt and black pepper and bake for about 20 minutes in a preheated oven at 200°C/Fan 180°C/Gas 6, covering the chicken with foil for the first 10 minutes. (Check the chicken is ready by slicing through the thickest part – there should be no pinkness remaining.)

A quick pasta dish with colourful vegetables and lean chicken breast coated in a light creamy sauce.

Half fill a large non-stick saucepan with water and bring it to the boil. Tip the pasta into the boiling water, stir well and return to the boil. Cook for 10 minutes, or according to the packet instructions, stirring occasionally until almost completely tender, or al dente.

Meanwhile, trim the bacon of any visible fat and cut it into 2cm-wide strips. Brush or spray a large non-stick frying pan with oil and place over a medium heat. Add the bacon and mushrooms and fry for 2 minutes or until lightly browned, stirring regularly. While the bacon is cooking, cut or tear the chicken into strips.

Add the tomatoes and chicken to the pan, season with salt and pepper and cook for 3–4 minutes more, stirring until the chicken is hot and the tomatoes are well softened.

When the pasta is al dente, add the broccoli to the saucepan and continue cooking for 2 minutes more. Drain the pasta and broccoli in a colander and return to the saucepan.

Add the bacon, mushrooms, chicken and tomatoes and pour over the cream. Toss together over a low heat for 1–2 minutes and serve.

343
CALORIES
PER SERVING

chicken tikka
and saffron rice

SERVES 4

PREP: 20 MINUTES,
PLUS MARINATING TIME

COOK: 20 MINUTES

4 boneless, skinless chicken
    breasts (each about 150g)
3 tbsp fat-free natural
    yoghurt
3 tbsp tikka curry paste
½ tsp flaked sea salt
lime wedges, fresh mint
    and coriander, to serve

FOR THE RICE AND
VEGETABLES
½ chicken stock cube
pinch of saffron strands
450ml just-boiled water
oil, for brushing or spraying
1 medium onion, thinly
    sliced
2 small red peppers,
    deseeded and cut into
    roughly 2cm chunks
1 tsp ground ginger
100g fine green beans,
    trimmed and halved
125g basmati rice
ground black pepper

Tip: Make a minted yoghurt
to serve alongside by
stirring 3 tablespoons of
finely chopped fresh mint
leaves into 150g of natural
yoghurt. Add small chunks
of cucumber too, if you like.
Serves 4 people with
24 calories per serving.

Succulent chicken tikka is very easy to prepare and goes
brilliantly with my saffron vegetable rice. If you don't have
any saffron, use half a teaspoon of ground turmeric. The rice
won't have the same flavour but it will have a lovely yellow
hue. You'll find tikka curry paste in the Indian section of the
supermarket or in Asian food stores. If not, use a medium curry
paste instead (not a curry sauce) – it will taste just as good.

To prepare the chicken, cut each chicken breast into 7–9 evenly
sized pieces and put the pieces in a bowl. Add the yoghurt and
curry paste, and season with the salt. Mix until well combined.
Cover and leave to marinate in the fridge for 1 hour.

To make the rice, put the stock cube and saffron in a measuring
jug and cover with the just-boiled water. Stir until the cube
dissolves. Leave to stand.

Spray or brush a large, wide-based, non-stick saucepan or
sauté pan with oil and cook the onion and peppers over a
medium-low heat for 5 minutes or until softened, stirring often.

Add the ginger and cook for 30 seconds more, stirring. Add the
green beans, saffron stock and rice, season with black pepper
and bring to the boil. Reduce the heat and cook for 10 minutes,
stirring occasionally until the rice is tender and almost all the
liquid has been absorbed. Remove the pan from the heat.
Cover with a clean tea towel and leave to stand for 5 minutes.

While the rice is cooking, preheat the grill to its hottest setting.
Thread the chicken onto long metal skewers and place them on
a rack over a grill pan or baking tray. Cook close to the grill for
5 minutes. Turn over and cook the other side for 4–5 minutes
or until lightly charred and cooked through. (There should be
no pink remaining.)

Fluff up the rice with a fork. Divide between 4 warmed plates
or deep bowls. Top with the chicken tikka, serve with yoghurt,
lime wedges, fresh mint and coriander.

367

CALORIES
PER SERVING

spaghetti bolognese

SERVES 6
PREP: 15 MINUTES
COOK: 50 MINUTES

500g lean minced beef
(10% fat or less)
1 medium onion, finely
chopped
2 celery sticks, trimmed
and thinly sliced
2 medium carrots, peeled
and finely diced
2 garlic cloves, crushed
250g baby button
mushrooms, halved
or quartered if large
100g dried red split lentils
125ml red wine or extra
stock
400g can chopped
tomatoes
2 tbsp tomato purée
1 tsp dried oregano
600ml cold water
1 beef stock cube
1 bay leaf
200g dried spaghetti
ground black pepper
flaked sea salt

Flat freeze the cooked
and cooled Bolognese
sauce in freezer bags for up
to 4 months. Rinse the bags
under hot water, break the
sauce into a wide-based,
non-stick saucepan, add a
splash of water and reheat,
stirring regularly until
piping hot throughout.

My spaghetti Bolognese is made with additional vegetables
and red lentils, so it's packed with extra fibre and vitamins.
Serve with a small portion of freshly cooked spaghetti and a
small sprinkling of Parmesan if you like. Don't forget to add an
additional 50 calories for every 10g of Parmesan you use.

Dry fry the mince with the onion, celery, carrots and garlic
in a large wide-based, non-stick saucepan or sauté pan over
a medium heat for about 5 minutes or until the beef is no longer
pink. Squash the meat with a wooden spoon to break up any
large lumps.

Add the mushrooms and fry them with the mince and
vegetables for a further 3 minutes, stirring regularly. Add the
lentils, wine or stock, tomatoes, tomato purée and oregano.
Pour the water into the pan. Crumble the stock cube over the
top, add the bay leaf, season with ground black pepper, give
it a good stir and bring to a simmer.

When the liquid is bubbling, cover the pan loosely with a lid
and leave to simmer over a low heat for 30 minutes, stirring
occasionally. Remove the lid and simmer uncovered for a
further 10–15 minutes, stirring occasionally until thickened
and saucy.

While the meat sauce is cooking, half fill a large saucepan
with water and bring it to the boil. Add the spaghetti, return
to the boil and cook for 10–12 minutes, or according to the
packet instructions, until tender, stirring occasionally. Drain
in a colander. Season the Bolognese to taste with salt and
pepper and serve with spaghetti.

384
CALORIES
PER SERVING

home-made meatballs with tagliatelle

SERVES 6

PREP: 30 MINUTES

COOK: 30 MINUTES

1 thick slice of wholemeal
 bread (about 50g)
4 tbsp semi-skimmed milk
1 small onion
2 medium carrots
 (each about 100g)
250g lean minced beef
 (10% or less fat)
250g minced pork (or extra
 beef mince)
2 tbsp finely chopped fresh
 oregano leaves, plus extra
 to serve (optional) or
 1 tsp dried oregano
1 large egg yolk
½ tsp fine sea salt
500g tomato and basil
 pasta sauce (from a jar)
275g dried egg tagliatelle
1 tsp olive oil
ground black pepper

Freeze the cooked and
cooled meatballs and sauce
in freezer-proof containers
for up to 4 months. Thaw
overnight in the fridge and
reheat in a saucepan or
microwave until piping
hot throughout.

Tip: If you have any leftover
mince, flat freeze it in
freezer bags for up to
3 months then cook from
frozen for Bolognese or
cottage pie, or defrost first
for burgers or meatballs.

**Home-made pork and beef meatballs are teamed with a
ready-made jar of tomato pasta sauce – look for one that's
made without heaps of additional oil. The combination of
meats and the addition of fresh bread and vegetables helps
keep the meatballs deliciously moist.**

To make the meatballs, cut the crusts off the bread, tear the
bread into rough pieces and put in a large bowl. Pour over the
milk and leave to soak for about 10 minutes. Preheat the oven
to 200°C/Fan 180°C/Gas 6.

Peel and finely grate the onion. Do the same with the carrot
(you will need about 150g grated carrot). Add the vegetables,
beef, pork, oregano and egg yolk to the bread and milk. Season
with the salt and lots of freshly ground black pepper and mix
thoroughly.

With clean hands, roll the mince mixture into 24 small balls
and place them on a large baking tray. Cook in the oven for
20 minutes or until lightly browned, taking them out and
turning after 10 minutes.

Take the baking tray out of the oven and transfer the meatballs
to a saucepan. Add the tomato pasta sauce and 200ml of
water. Bring to a gentle simmer, stirring. Cook for 10 minutes
more, or until the meatballs are piping hot throughout.

While the meatballs are cooking, half fill a large saucepan
with water and bring it to the boil. Add the tagliatelle and
cook for 8–10 minutes, or according to the packet instructions,
until tender.

Drain the pasta in a colander then toss with the olive oil and
season with ground black pepper. Tip it onto a warmed serving
dish and top with the meatballs and sauce. Garnish with fresh
oregano, if using, and serve sprinkled with a little freshly grated
Parmesan, but don't forget to add the extra calories. Serve with
a large mixed salad.

444

frying pan beef lasagne

SERVES 5

PREP: 20 MINUTES

COOK: 50 MINUTES

500g lean minced beef
(10% fat or less)
1 medium onion,
finely chopped
2 celery sticks, trimmed
and thinly sliced
2 medium carrots, peeled
and diced
2 garlic cloves, crushed
200g button chestnut
mushrooms, halved
or quartered if large
125ml red wine
400g can chopped
tomatoes
2 tbsp tomato purée
1 beef stock cube
1 bay leaf
1 tsp dried oregano
4 sheets fresh lasagne
(each about 35g)
25g Parmesan cheese,
finely grated
½ tsp paprika (not smoked)
250g tub ricotta cheese
50g ready-grated
mozzarella cheese
(from a packet)
ground black pepper

This all-in-one lasagne can be made in one pan and doesn't
need to be baked. I like to use a deep frying pan or a sauté pan
with a wide base. You can use dried lasagne sheets if you like,
but you will need to cook them first as the final cooking time
is fairly short. These quantities make five generous portions
or six smaller portions. Serve with a colourful mixed salad.

Dry fry the mince with the onion, celery and carrots in
a large non-stick sauté pan, large deep frying pan or shallow
flameproof casserole over a medium heat for about 5 minutes
or until the beef is no longer pink. Squash the meat with a
wooden spoon to break up any large lumps.

Add the garlic and mushrooms and fry with the mince and
vegetables for a further 2–3 minutes. Stir in the wine, tomatoes
and tomato purée. Refill the tomato can with cold water and
pour the water into the pan.

Crumble the stock cube over the top, add the bay leaf and
oregano, season with ground black pepper, give everything
a good stir and bring to a simmer. When the liquid is bubbling,
cover the pan loosely with a lid and leave to simmer over a low
heat for 30 minutes, stirring occasionally.

While the sauce is simmering, half fill a large mixing bowl with
just-boiled water from the kettle. Cut the lasagne sheets in half
widthways and stir them into the water one at a time. Leave
to soak for 10 minutes. Mix the Parmesan and paprika together
in a small bowl.

Drain the lasagne sheets and then add them to the mince
mixture, one at a time. Stir until loosely combined. Place
dessertspoonfuls of the ricotta on top and sprinkle with the
mozzarella and then the paprika and Parmesan mixture. Cook
very gently for a further 10 minutes, without stirring, or until the
ricotta is hot and the mozzarella has melted.

416
CALORIES
PER SERVING

simple tagliatelle carbonara

SERVES 2
PREP: 15 MINUTES
COOK: 12-15 MINUTES

100g dried tagliatelle
50g frozen peas
oil, for brushing or spraying
2 smoked back bacon
   rashers, trimmed of fat
   and cut into roughly
   1.5cm wide strips
100g baby button
   mushrooms, halved or
   quartered if large
1 large courgette, trimmed,
   halved lengthways and
   cut into 1cm slices
50ml double cream
25g Parmesan cheese,
   finely grated
flaked sea salt
ground black pepper

Tip: I used spinach tagliatelle for this photo but you can use any long pasta you like. Linguine, fettuccine and spaghetti all work well.

A very easy pasta dish for two. I've used both full-fat cheese and cream, but kept the quantities reasonably low and increased the vegetables to help fill you up. Use single cream if you want to reduce the calories even further.

Half fill a large saucepan with water and bring it to the boil. Tip the pasta into the boiling water and cook for 6–8 minutes, or according to the packet instructions, until tender. Add the frozen peas after 5 minutes.

Meanwhile, spray or brush a large non-stick frying pan or wok with oil and place the pan over a high heat. Add the bacon and mushrooms, season well with salt and pepper and stir-fry for 2 minutes.

Add the courgette and stir-fry for a further 2–3 minutes, until tender and lightly browned. Drain the pasta and peas in a colander then return them to the pan. Add the bacon and mushrooms, cream and half the Parmesan. Toss well together with a couple of forks until evenly mixed and warm through gently for about a minute. Season with more ground black pepper and serve with the rest of the grated Parmesan.

373
CALORIES
PER SERVING

sausage pasta pot

SERVES 4
PREP: 10 MINUTES
COOK: 35 MINUTES

1 tbsp sunflower oil
6 lean pork sausages
1 large onion, thinly sliced
1 yellow pepper, deseeded
    and cut into roughly
    3cm chunks
1 medium courgette, halved
    lengthways and cut into
    roughly 2cm slices
2 garlic cloves, crushed
1/4 tsp dried chilli flakes
1 tsp dried oregano
400g can chopped
    tomatoes with herbs
150g dried penne
2 tbsp tomato purée
600ml chicken or pork
    stock (made with
    1 stock cube)
flaked sea salt
ground black pepper
flat-leaf parsley, to garnish
    (optional)

Freeze the cooked and
cooled pasta pot in freezer-
proof containers for up to
2 months. Thaw overnight
in the fridge and reheat
in a large non-stick
saucepan with a splash of
water, or microwave,
stirring regularly, until
piping hot throughout.

Dried pasta will cook in a casserole if you allow a bit of extra
time, so this one pot dish will feed a hungry family and save
on washing up.

Heat the oil in a large wide-based, non-stick saucepan, sauté
pan or flameproof casserole and fry the sausages gently for
10 minutes, turning them every now and then until they are
browned all over. Transfer to a plate and set aside.

Put the onion and pepper in the same pan and fry over a
medium heat for 3 minutes until they are beginning to soften,
stirring often. Add the courgette, garlic, chilli flakes and
oregano and cook for 2 minutes more, stirring.

Stir in the tomatoes, pasta, tomato purée and stock. Bring to
a simmer. Reduce the heat slightly and leave to simmer gently
for 15 minutes, stirring every now and then.

Cut each sausage into 3 pieces then return them to the pan
and cook everything for a further 2–3 minutes or until the pasta
is tender and the sausages are hot. Stir regularly and add a little
extra water if necessary. Season well with salt and pepper and
garnish with chopped parsley, if using, just before serving.

261
CALORIES
PER SERVING

pasta puttanesca

SERVES 4
PREP: 10 MINUTES
COOK: 25 MINUTES

1 tbsp olive oil
6 anchovy fillets in olive oil
 (from a jar or can),
 drained
3 garlic cloves, very thinly
 sliced
½ small onion, very finely
 chopped
400g can chopped
 tomatoes
2 tbsp tomato purée
100g pitted black olives,
 drained and halved
25g capers (from a jar),
 drained
1 tsp dried chilli flakes
200g dried spaghetti
ground black pepper
handful of fresh flat-leaf
 parsley, leaves roughly
 chopped (optional)

Flat freeze the cooked and
cooled pasta with the sauce
in zip-sealed bags for up to
1 month. Thaw overnight in
the fridge and reheat in the
microwave or a non-stick
saucepan with a splash of
water, stirring regularly until
piping hot throughout.

Also known as 'tart's spaghetti', this dish can be made using mainly store cupboard ingredients plus onion and garlic, so it's a great recipe when you have nothing planned. It's packed with bold, Italian flavours and a little goes a long way.

Heat the oil in a large non-stick frying pan and cook the anchovies, garlic and onion for 3–4 minutes over a low heat until well softened, stirring regularly until the anchovies break up and become mushy.

Stir in the tomatoes, tomato purée, olives, capers and chilli flakes and cook over a low heat for 18–20 minutes, stirring regularly until the sauce is hot and thick.

While the sauce is cooking, half fill a large saucepan with water and bring it to the boil. Cook the pasta for 10–12 minutes or according to the packet instructions until tender, stirring regularly. Drain well and return to the saucepan.

Tip the puttanesca sauce into the pan with the pasta. Season with ground black pepper and toss together well. Garnish with parsley if you like and serve with a large mixed salad.

317
CALORIES
PER SERVING

cauliflower macaroni cheese

SERVES 4

PREP: 15 MINUTES

COOK: 40–45 MINUTES

275g small cauliflower florets

150g dried macaroni or other small pasta shapes

25g butter, plus extra for greasing

25g plain flour

300ml semi-skimmed milk

50g mature Cheddar cheese, finely grated

100g cherry or small tomatoes, halved or quartered if large

flaked sea salt

ground black pepper

Freeze the cooked and cooled pasta in single servings, in freezer-proof containers for up to 1 month. Thaw overnight in the fridge and reheat in the microwave, stirring ocasionally until piping hot throughout.

Tips: It's most cost effective to buy a whole cauliflower and then cut off the florets needed for this recipe. A 700g cauliflower with leaves will provide about 275g of florets.

If you don't have a stick blender, blitz the cauliflower thoroughly in a food processor after cooling for a few minutes, or press the sauce through a sieve.

Puréed cauliflower is my secret ingredient when it comes to making creamy tasting sauces without the cream! And it's a great way of adding extra vegetables to your cooking.

Preheat the oven to 200°C/Fan 180°C/Gas 6. Half fill a large saucepan with water and bring it to the boil. Add the cauliflower and return to the boil. Cook for 10–12 minutes or until very soft. Drain in a colander.

Half fill a second pan with water and bring it to the boil. Add the macaroni and cook for 8–10 minutes, or according to the packet instructions, until tender, stirring occasionally.

While the pasta is cooking, prepare the sauce. Melt the butter in a large non-stick saucepan over a low heat then add in the flour and cook for 30 seconds, stirring continuously.

Gradually add the milk, stirring well and cooking for a few seconds before adding more. Bring to a gentle simmer and cook for 3-5 minutes or until the sauce is thickened and smooth, stirring continuously. Season with a little salt and some ground black pepper. Remove from the hob.

Add the cooked cauliflower to the pan with the sauce. Using a stick blender, blitz the cauliflower into the sauce until it is as smooth as possible. Return to the hob and warm through gently, adding a little more seasoning or a dash of milk if necessary. It should have the consistency of pouring custard.

Drain the pasta in a large colander and tip it into the cauliflower sauce. Mix them lightly together then transfer the mixture to a shallow 2-litre ovenproof dish – a lasagne dish is ideal. Sprinkle with the cheese, top with cherry tomatoes and lots of freshly ground black pepper, and bake for 20–25 minutes or until golden brown and bubbling.

314 CALORIES PER SERVING

veggie bolognese

SERVES 6

PREP: 10 MINUTES

COOK: 40 MINUTES

1 tbsp sunflower oil
1 medium onion, finely
    chopped
2 garlic cloves, crushed
2 medium carrots, peeled
    and finely grated
1 medium courgette,
    finely grated
1 red pepper, deseeded
    and finely diced
250g sachet of cooked
    puy lentils
150g dried split red lentils
2 large portobello
    mushrooms, peeled
    and roughly chopped
400g can chopped
    tomatoes
800ml cold water
2 tbsp tomato purée
1 tsp dried oregano
    or mixed dried herbs
1 vegetable stock cube
1 bay leaf
200g dried spaghetti
flaked sea salt
ground black pepper

Flat freeze the cooked and
cooled Bolognese sauce
in freezer bags for up to
4 months. Rinse the bags
under hot water, break the
sauce into a wide-based
saucepan, add a splash of
water and reheat, stirring,
until piping hot throughout.

This rich veggie Bolognese uses lots of lovely vegetables and makes four generous servings or six small portions. It freezes really well and can be used for a lasagne or pasta bake, or even a base for cottage pie if you like. Use 100g of dried puy lentils if you prefer and increase the water by 100ml.

Heat the oil in a large, wide-based, non-stick saucepan or sauté pan and gently fry the onion, garlic, carrots, courgette and pepper for 10 minutes or until softened, stirring regularly.

Add all the lentils, the mushrooms, tomatoes, water, tomato purée, oregano or mixed herbs, the stock cube and bay leaf. Season with salt and pepper and bring to a gentle simmer.

Cook for about 30 minutes or until the red lentils have completely softened and become mushy and thick. The puy lentils will retain much of their texture. Stir occasionally at the beginning and more regularly towards the end of the cooking time.

While the sauce is cooking, half fill a large saucepan with water and bring it to the boil. Add the spaghetti, return to the boil and cook for 10–12 minutes, or according to the packet instructions, until tender, stirring occasionally. Drain in a colander.

Season the Bolognese with ground black pepper and serve with the spaghetti or any other pasta.

roast vegetable, goat's cheese and sun-dried tomato pasta

SERVES 5
PREP: 15 MINUTES
COOK: 30 MINUTES

1 red pepper, deseeded
   and cut into roughly
   2cm chunks
1 yellow pepper, deseeded
   and cut into roughly
   2cm chunks
300g sweet potato, peeled
   and cut into roughly
   2cm chunks
2 medium courgettes, cut
   into roughly 1.5cm slices
1 medium red onion, cut
   into 10 thin wedges
1 tbsp sunflower or mild
   olive oil
½ tsp dried chilli flakes
   (optional)
3 sun-dried tomato pieces,
   drained, halved and
   cut into thin strips
1 tbsp pine nuts
200g dried pasta shapes,
   such as farfalle
20g fresh basil leaves,
   plus extra to garnish
75g soft goat's cheese,
   cut into small chunks
flaked sea salt
ground black pepper

Tip: If your courgettes are fairly large, cut them in half lengthways before slicing.

A colourful medley of roasted vegetables with tangy goat's cheese and sweet sun-dried tomatoes. If you leave out the goat's cheese, you can save 28 calories per serving but I love its creamy texture and think it complements the other ingredients beautifully.

Preheat the oven to 220°C/Fan 200°C/Gas 7. Put all the vegetables in a bowl and toss with the oil. Season with a good pinch of salt and ground black pepper. Scatter the vegetables over a baking tray in a single layer and roast them for 20 minutes.

Add the chilli flakes, sun-dried tomatoes and pine nuts to the tray, turn the vegetables and return the tray to the oven for a further 10 minutes. The vegetables should be softened and lightly browned when they are done.

While the vegetables are roasting, half fill a large saucepan with water and bring it to the boil. Add the pasta to the pan and cook for 10–12 minutes, or according to the packet instructions, until tender. Drain the pasta in a colander then return it to the saucepan.

Take the tray out of the oven and carefully add the vegetables to the pasta. Season with ground black pepper and toss together until evenly mixed. Tear the basil leaves on top and add the cheese, toss very lightly and serve in deep bowls, garnished with extra basil.

340
CALORIES
PER SERVING

blue cheese and spinach rigatoni

SERVES 4
PREP: 15 MINUTES
COOK: 25–30 MINUTES

275g small cauliflower
   florets
175g dried rigatoni or other
   small pasta shapes
25g butter, plus extra for
   greasing
25g plain flour
300ml semi-skimmed milk
100g young spinach leaves
50g soft blue cheese, such
   as Roquefort
flaked sea salt
ground black pepper

Tip: If you don't have a stick blender, blitz the cauliflower thoroughly in a food processor after cooling for a few minutes or press the sauce through a sieve.

My magical cauliflower sauce makes the sauce for this rigatoni taste wonderfully rich and creamy, but it's actually made with semi-skimmed milk and only a little butter. A 700g cauliflower with leaves should yield enough florets for this recipe, or try using frozen florets if you prefer.

Half fill a large saucepan with water and bring it to the boil. Add the cauliflower, return to the boil and cook for 10–12 minutes or until very soft.

Half fill a second pan with water and bring it to the boil. Add the pasta and cook for 8–10 minutes, or according to the packet instructions, stirring occasionally until tender.

While the pasta is cooking, prepare the sauce. Melt the butter in a medium non-stick saucepan over a low heat then add the flour and cook for 30 seconds, stirring continuously.

Gradually stir in the milk and bring to a gentle simmer. Cook for 3-5 minutes or until the sauce is thickened and smooth, stirring continuously. Season with a little salt and some ground black pepper. Remove from the hob.

Add the cooked cauliflower to the pan with the sauce. Using a stick blender, blitz the cauliflower into the sauce until it is as smooth as possible. Return to the hob and warm through gently, adding a little more seasoning or a dash of milk if necessary. It should have the consistency of pouring custard.

Stir the spinach into the pasta pan and simmer for a few seconds until softened. Drain the pasta and spinach in a large colander and return to the pan. Add the cauliflower sauce and the blue cheese, broken into small pieces, and toss lightly. Serve with a lightly dressed salad.

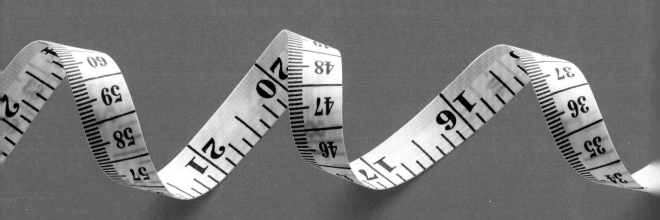

risotto
and pilaf

354
CALORIES
PER SERVING

chicken, mushroom and pea risotto

SERVES 4

PREP: 10 MINUTES

COOK: 25 MINUTES

1 tbsp olive oil
150g small chestnut
  mushrooms, sliced
1 medium onion, finely
  chopped
3 boneless, skinless chicken
  breasts (each about
  150g), trimmed and cut
  into roughly 2.5cm chunks
2 garlic cloves, crushed
150g Arborio (risotto) rice
100ml white wine or extra
  chicken stock
850ml hot chicken stock
  (made with 1 chicken
  stock cube)
25g Parmesan cheese, finely
  grated, plus extra to serve
100g frozen peas
flaked sea salt
ground black pepper

This is one of my family's favourite risottos and it's so easy. It's made by adding all of the stock at once rather than being stirred in gradually, which means you can get on with other things while the risotto is cooking, and just nip back every now and then for a quick stir.

Place a large non-stick saucepan on the hob over a medium-high heat and add the oil. Fry the sliced mushrooms for 3 minutes until lightly browned, stirring continuously.

Add the onion and chicken to the pan and cook them with the mushrooms for a further 3–5 minutes until pale golden brown, stirring. Add the garlic and the rice and cook for a few seconds, stirring. Stir in the wine, if using, and bubble for a few seconds.

Add all the stock and bring to a simmer. Cook for 15 minutes, stirring frequently until the rice looks swollen and creamy and almost all the stock has been absorbed. The risotto should look fairly saucy at this point, so if yours appears quite thick, stir in some extra water.

Add the Parmesan and the peas and heat through for 2–3 minutes until the peas are hot, stirring continuously. Remove the pan from the heat and adjust the seasoning to taste. Sprinkle with a little more Parmesan to serve, but don't forget to add an extra 50 calories for each 10g you use. Serve with a mixed salad.

448

hunter's risotto

SERVES 4
PREP: 15 MINUTES
COOK: 35 MINUTES

1 tbsp sunflower oil
1 medium onion, finely
  chopped
1 celery stick, thinly sliced
1 medium carrot, peeled and
  cut into roughly 1cm dice
6 boneless, skinless chicken
  thighs (about 500g)
2 large Portobello
  mushrooms, trimmed
  and thickly sliced
2 rashers of smoked back
  bacon, trimmed of fat and
  cut into 2cm-wide strips
2 garlic cloves, crushed
200g Arborio (risotto) rice
1 large bay leaf
small bunch of fresh thyme
  (3–4 sprigs)
100ml Marsala or Madeira
  wine
800ml hot chicken stock
  (made with 1 chicken
  stock cube)
25g Parmesan cheese,
  grated
chopped fresh parsley,
  to garnish (optional)
flaked sea salt
ground black pepper

I call this hunter's risotto because it contains all the ingredients I add to hunter's chicken, or chicken chasseur, as it is known in France. It's made extra rich by the addition of Marsala or Madeira wine, but you could add sweet sherry, Martini Rosso or even red wine if you prefer.

Heat the oil in a large wide-based, non-stick saucepan or sauté pan and fry the onion, celery and carrot for 10 minutes over a low heat, stirring.

Trim the chicken of excess fat and cut each thigh into 6 pieces. Add the chicken, mushrooms and bacon to the pan and cook over a high heat for 5–8 minutes or until the chicken is lightly browned, stirring regularly. Season with salt and pepper, add the garlic and cook for a few seconds more, stirring.

Add the rice, bay leaf and thyme sprigs and stir for a few seconds before adding the Marsala or Madeira. Allow to bubble for a few seconds more, then start adding the stock, a ladleful at a time, stirring well after each addition. Don't add more until the previous ladleful has been almost all absorbed by the rice and keep stirring.

You'll need to cook the risotto for 15-20 minutes, or until the rice is tender and the risotto is creamy, rich and dark, stirring regularly. (Add a little extra water if necessary until the right consistency is reached – don't forget that it will thicken as it sits.) Stir in the Parmesan and season to taste with salt and pepper. Garnish with chopped parsley, if using, and serve with a large rocket salad if you like.

458
CALORIES
PER SERVING

persian lamb pilaf

SERVES 6
PREP: 25 MINUTES
COOK: 2¼ HOURS

100ml semi-skimmed milk
couple pinches of saffron
finely grated zest of
 1 orange
3 medium onions, peeled
3 garlic cloves, peeled
20g chunk of fresh root
 ginger, peeled and
 roughly chopped
1 plump fresh red chilli,
 roughly chopped (deseed
 first if you like)
3 tsp ras-el-hanout
2 tsp flaked sea salt,
 plus extra to season
50ml cold water, plus
 200ml
800g lean lamb leg steaks,
 trimmed and cut into
 roughly 3cm chunks
2½ tbsp sunflower oil
100g fat-free natural
 yoghurt, plus extra
 to serve
2 bay leaves
10 cardamom pods,
 lightly crushed
1 cinnamon stick, broken
 in half
200g basmati rice
25g sultanas
15g flaked almonds,
 preferably toasted
20g bunch of fresh
 coriander, leaves roughly
 chopped, plus extra
 to garnish
75g ready-to-eat dried
 apricots, quartered
ground black pepper

This lamb pilaf is packed with Middle Eastern flavours and makes a stunning centrepiece when taken to the table.

Heat the milk, saffron threads and orange zest in a small saucepan for 2–3 minutes without boiling; set aside. Roughly chop 2 onions and blend to a paste in a food processor with the garlic, ginger, chilli, ras-el-hanout, 1 teaspoon of salt and 50ml of cold water.

Preheat the oven to 180°C/Fan 160°C/Gas 4. Put the lamb in a bowl, season and toss with 1 tablespoon of oil. Brown in a large non-stick frying pan in 2–3 batches over a medium-high heat then tip into a large heavy-based flameproof casserole.

Add 1 tablespoon of oil to the frying pan and cook the spiced onion paste over a medium heat for 5 minutes or until lightly browned, stirring often and adding extra water if needed. Tip into the casserole with the lamb. Stir in the yoghurt, the remaining 200ml water and the bay leaves. Place over a low heat and bring to a simmer, stirring regularly. Cover with a lid and cook in the oven for 1½ hours or until the lamb is tender.

Cut the remaining onion in half and slice thinly. Heat ½ tablespoon of oil in a large non-stick frying pan and cook the onion for 6–8 minutes over a fairly high heat until browned, stirring frequently. Tip onto a plate covered in kitchen paper and leave to drain.

Half fill a large pan with water, add the second teaspoon of salt, the cardamom pods and cinnamon stick and bring to the boil. Rinse the rice in a sieve, add to the pan and return to the boil. Cook for 5 minutes then drain well and return to the saucepan. Add the sultanas, almonds and chopped coriander.

Take the lamb out of the oven and stir in the apricots. The sauce should be thick and the lamb tender. Spoon over the part cooked rice and drizzle with the soaked saffron threads, orange zest and milk. Scatter with the fried onions. Cover the surface with baking parchment then replace the lid and bake for 25 minutes. Garnish with coriander and serve with a large salad and yoghurt.

319
CALORIES
PER SERVING

ham and leek risotto

SERVES 4
PREP: 10 MINUTES
COOK: 25 MINUTES

1 tbsp sunflower oil
1 small onion, finely chopped
2 medium leeks, trimmed and cut into roughly 1cm slices
2 garlic cloves, very thinly sliced
200g Arborio (risotto) rice
100ml white wine or dry vermouth, or extra stock
800ml hot vegetable or chicken stock (made with 1 stock cube)
50g mature Cheddar cheese, finely grated
100g sliced ham, preferably smoked, cut into roughly 2cm-wide strips
flaked sea salt
ground black pepper

I love this risotto, probably because it's incredibly simple to make, yet tastes superb. It also uses ingredients that you may well already have in your fridge and is very easy to adapt.

Place a large non-stick saucepan over a medium-high heat and add the oil. Fry the onion and leeks for 5 minutes or until they are beginning to soften, stirring regularly. Add the garlic and rice and cook for a few seconds more, stirring. Add the white wine or vermouth and let it bubble for a few seconds.

Reduce the heat to medium-low, add a large ladleful of the hot stock to the pan and stir well. As soon as it has been absorbed, add another. Continue gradually stirring the stock into the rice until it has all been absorbed and the rice looks swollen and creamy. It should be very tender with just the merest hint of a bite.

Add the Cheddar and ham and cook for 3–5 minutes more, stirring well and adding a little extra water if needed. Season with salt and pepper then divide the risotto between 4 warmed deep plates or bowls. Serve with a large mixed salad.

asparagus and lemon risotto

SERVES 2
PREP: 10 MINUTES
COOK: 22 MINUTES

2 tsp olive oil
½ medium onion, finely chopped
2 garlic cloves, crushed
100g Arborio (risotto) rice
50ml white wine or extra stock
600ml hot vegetable or chicken stock (made with 1 stock cube)
125g thin asparagus spears, trimmed and halved widthways
25g Parmesan or Grano Padano cheese, finely grated
finely grated zest and juice of 1 lemon
flaked sea salt
ground black pepper

A zingy, fresh-tasting risotto that makes a perfect lunch or light supper. Add 125g of frozen peas instead of the asparagus if you like.

Place a medium non-stick saucepan over a medium heat and add the oil. Gently fry the onion for 5 minutes or until softened and lightly browned, stirring regularly. Add the garlic and rice and cook for 30 seconds, stirring. Add the wine and bubble for a few seconds.

Reduce the heat to medium-low, add a third of the stock and stir well. Bring the liquid to a gentle simmer and cook for 5 minutes, stirring regularly. Add half the remaining stock and simmer for 5 minutes more, stirring regularly. Add the remaining stock and cook for 5 minutes more, stirring. The rice should be almost tender at this point but very saucy. Add more stock if needed.

While the rice is cooking, half fill a medium saucepan with water and bring it to the boil. Add the asparagus, return the water to the boil and cook for 1-2 minutes or until just tender. Drain the asparagus in a colander.

When the rice has been cooking for 15 minutes, stir in the cheese and season well with salt and pepper. Add the asparagus and lemon zest and juice. Cook over a low heat for 2 minutes more or until the rice is tender and the asparagus is hot.

329
CALORIES
PER SERVING

roast squash, spinach and sage risotto

SERVES 5
PREP: 15 MINUTES
COOK: 35 MINUTES

1 small–medium butternut
squash (about 1kg)
2 tbsp sunflower oil
½ tsp dried chilli flakes
1 medium onion,
finely chopped
2 garlic cloves, very
thinly sliced
200g Arborio (risotto) rice
100ml Marsala or Madeira
wine, or extra stock
750ml hot vegetable or
chicken stock (made
with 1 stock cube)
50g Parmesan or Grano
Padano cheese,
finely grated
150g young spinach leaves
15g fresh sage leaves
flaked sea salt
ground black pepper

Tip: The risotto will cook
in about 20 minutes and
you will need to stir the
rice regularly. It should look
fairly saucy at the end, so
if yours appears quite thick,
stir in some extra water.

Don't eat the squash skin
as it will be quite tough.
Simply scrape the soft,
sweet flesh from the skin
as you eat the risotto.

Creamy tasting spinach risotto topped with sweet, roasted butternut squash and crispy sage leaves makes a filling and colourful supper or weekend lunch. Serve with a lightly dressed side salad.

Preheat the oven to 200°C/Fan 180°C/Gas 6. Cut the squash in half lengthways and scoop out the seeds. Cut the halves into roughly 1.5cm slices and put them in a large bowl. Add 1 tablespoon of the oil, salt and a good grind of black pepper and toss well together.

Scatter the squash pieces over a medium roasting tin, in a single layer, and bake for 20 minutes. Turn the squash over, sprinkle with the chilli flakes and bake for a further 10 minutes or until tender and nicely browned. Take the tin out of the oven.

While the squash is cooking, prepare the risotto. Place a large non-stick saucepan over a medium-high heat and add the remaining oil. Fry the onion for 5 minutes or until it is beginning to soften. Add the garlic and rice and cook for 30 seconds, stirring. Add the Marsala or Madeira and let it bubble for a few seconds.

Reduce the heat to medium-low, add a large ladleful of hot stock to the pan and stir well. As soon as it has been absorbed, add another. Continue gradually stirring the stock into the rice until it has all been used and the rice looks swollen and creamy.

Add the Parmesan and spinach, season with salt and pepper and cook for 3 minutes more, stirring well. Meanwhile, sprinkle the sage leaves over the squash and return it to the oven for 5 minutes or until crisp. Divide the risotto between 5 plates. Top each pile of risotto with warm roasted squash and sage leaves.

79
CALORIES
PER BALL

oven-baked arancini

MAKES 14

**PREP: 20 MINUTES,
PLUS CHILLING TIME**

COOK: 50 MINUTES

15g dried porcini
mushrooms
100ml just-boiled water
oil for spraying
1 small onion, finely
chopped
1 medium courgette (about
150g), cut into roughly
1cm chunks
100g small chestnut
mushrooms, roughly
chopped
2 garlic cloves, crushed
200g Arborio (risotto) rice
400ml chicken or vegetable
stock (made with 1 stock
cube)
15g bunch flat-leaf parsley,
leaves finely chopped
4 small slices wholemeal
bread (about 115g)
1 large egg
1 tsp ground paprika
(not smoked)
flaked sea salt
ground black pepper

Tip: Use a pasta sauce to
drizzle or dip the arancini.
Look for a sauce that
contains about 50 calories
per 100g. Heat through
gently in a small saucepan.

**Arancini are small balls of cold, cooked risotto rolled in
breadcrumbs and deep-fried. My risotto is made using as little
fat as possible, then rolled in brown breadcrumbs and baked
until crisp.**

Put the dried mushrooms in a measuring jug and cover with
the just-boiled water. Leave to stand. Spray a large non-stick
saucepan with oil and place over a medium heat. Cook the
onion, courgette and fresh mushrooms for 5 minutes or until
softened, stirring frequently. Add the garlic and rice and cook
for 1 minute more, stirring.

Pour over the stock, bring to a simmer and cook the rice
for 15 minutes, stirring regularly. Strain the softened dried
mushrooms, reserving the liquor, and roughly chop. Add the
reserved liquor and soaked mushroom to the risotto and cook
for 5 minutes more, or until the rice is tender and creamy. Add
a splash more water if the sauce thickens before the rice is
ready. Spread the rice mixture onto a baking tray lined with
cling film and cool for 20 minutes. Cover and put in the fridge
for a further 40 minutes or until solid.

Preheat the oven to 220°C/Fan 200°C/Gas 7. Tip the rice
mixture into a bowl and stir in the parsley. Season with salt and
pepper and mix well. Roll the risotto into 14 small balls. If you
wet your hands with cold water, the rice won't stick. Cut the
crusts off the bread and blitz into crumbs with the paprika in
a food processor. Sprinkle half the crumbs onto a plate. Beat
the egg in a bowl. Spray a baking tray with oil.

Dip each of the rice balls in the egg and coat lightly in the
breadcrumbs. (Replace the crumbs after coating 7 balls.) Place
the risotto balls on the prepared tray and spray all over with oil.
Bake for 10 minutes then take the tray out of the oven and turn
the balls. Spray with more oil and return to the oven for a further
8-10 minutes or until golden brown and hot throughout. Serve
with a fresh tomato salsa or warm tomato pasta sauce.

358
CALORIES
PER SERVING

skinny kedgeree

SERVES 4

PREP: 15 MINUTES

COOK: 25 MINUTES

600ml cold water
400g smoked haddock
   fillets (unskinned)
oil, for brushing or spraying
1 medium onion,
   finely chopped
2 medium courgettes,
   halved lengthways
   and cut into roughly
   1.5cm slices
150g easy-cook, long
   grain rice
1 tbsp medium or mild
   curry powder
¼ tsp ground turmeric
4 medium eggs (fridge
   cold)
100g cherry tomatoes,
   halved
flaked sea salt
ground black pepper
chopped fresh parsley
   or coriander, to garnish

This classic combination of smoked fish with lightly curried rice makes a great brunch or supper dish. I've kept the calories as low as possible by omitting butter and cream and adding extra vegetables. If you leave out the eggs, you'll reduce the calories by a further 80 per serving.

Pour 600ml of cold water into a large saucepan and add the fish, skin-side up. (Cut the fillets in half if necessary so they fit.) Bring to a simmer and immediately turn off the heat. Leave the fish to poach for 5 minutes. Remove the fish from the water with a slotted spatula and leave to drain. Pour the poaching water into a wide-necked jug.

Brush or spray a large, deep frying or sauté pan with oil and place over a medium heat. Add the chopped onion and courgettes and fry for 6–8 minutes or until softened and beginning to brown. Boil a kettle of water. Stir the rice into the pan with the onion and sprinkle over the curry powder and turmeric. Cook for a few seconds more, stirring.

Pour over the reserved poaching water. Bring to a simmer and cook for 8 minutes, stirring occasionally until the rice is almost tender and the liquid has been absorbed.

While the rice is simmering, half fill a medium pan with just-boiled water and return to the boil. Gently add the eggs and return to the boil. Cook for 8 minutes then drain. Strip the skin off the haddock and discard it. Flake the flesh into chunky pieces discarding any stray bones.

Stir the fish and tomatoes gently through the rice and warm through over a low heat for 2–3 minutes or until the fish is hot and the tomatoes begin to soften. Meanwhile, peel the eggs and cut them into quarters. Place the eggs on top of the rice, scatter over a few parsley or coriander leaves and serve.

178
CALORIES
PER SERVING

pilau rice

SERVES 4
PREP: 10 MINUTES
COOK: 20 MINUTES

5 cardamom pods
1 tsp coriander seeds
½ tsp cumin seeds
2 tsp sunflower oil
½ medium onion,
    finely chopped
2 garlic cloves, finely
    chopped
½ cinnamon stick
2 bay leaves
175g basmati rice
1 tbsp medium curry
    powder
350ml hot chicken or
    vegetable stock (made
    with ½ stock cube)
½ tsp fine sea salt
ground black pepper

Tip: Whole spices make the dish look more appetising but don't eat the cardamom husks or cinnamon when it is served, as they are for flavouring only.

A quick and lower fat version of my pilau rice using curry powder rather than a host of different ground spices. Serve with home-made curries, tikka and tandoori style dishes or with plainly grilled or baked meat and fish.

Put the cardamom pods, coriander and cumin seeds in a pestle and mortar and pound lightly for a few seconds until the spices are lightly crushed.

Heat the oil over a low heat in a non-stick sauté pan or wide-based saucepan with a tight-fitting lid. Add the onion and garlic and fry for about 3 minutes or until softened and very lightly coloured, stirring regularly.

Sprinkle all the spices from the pestle and mortar into the pan, plus the cinnamon stick and bay leaves, and fry gently for 1 minute, stirring continuously.

Rinse the rice in a sieve under cold water for a few seconds to help remove excess starch. Stir the curry powder and rice into the onion mixture and cook for 30 seconds, stirring.

Pour over the stock. Add the salt and a good grind of black pepper. Stir well and bring to the boil. Give a final stir then cover the pan with a tight-fitting lid. Reduce the heat to its lowest setting and cook the rice for 12 minutes. The liquid should barely bubble.

Turn off the heat, remove the lid and quickly fluff up the rice with a fork, taking care not to break up the grains.

mushroom rice

SERVES 5
PREP: 10 MINUTES
COOK: 18–20 MINUTES

6 cardamom pods
1 tsp cumin seeds
¼ tsp black mustard seeds
25g butter
1 tsp sunflower oil
250g small chestnut
   mushrooms, thickly sliced
1 medium onion, thinly
   sliced
1 garlic clove, thinly sliced
10g chunk of fresh root
   ginger, peeled and
   finely grated
200g basmati rice
450ml cold water
1 tsp flaked sea salt
ground black pepper
fresh coriander leaves,
   to garnish (optional)

Tip: Whole spices make the dish look more appetising but don't eat the cardamom husks when it is served, as they are for flavouring only.

A simple savoury rice that goes well with grilled meat and fish as well as vegetarian and meat or chicken curries. Make sure you brown the mushrooms well before adding the other ingredients – they will add lots of flavour.

Put the cardamom pods and cumin seeds in a pestle and mortar and pound lightly for a few seconds until the spices are lightly crushed. Add the mustard seeds and set aside.

Melt the butter with the oil over a medium heat in a non-stick sauté pan or wide-based saucepan with a tight-fitting lid. Add the mushrooms and fry for 2–3 minutes or until nicely browned, stirring regularly.

Add the onion and cook for 2 minutes more. Stir in the garlic, ginger and spices, reduce the heat and cook gently for 1 minute more, stirring continuously.

Rinse the rice in a sieve under cold water for a few seconds to help remove excess starch. Add the rice to the mushroom mixture and cook for 30 seconds, stirring.

Pour over the water. Add the salt and a good grind of black pepper. Stir well and bring to the boil. Give a final stir then cover the pan with a tight-fitting lid. Reduce the heat to its lowest setting and cook the rice for 12 minutes. The liquid should barely bubble.

Turn off the heat, remove the lid and quickly fluff up the rice with a fork, taking care not to break up the grains. Garnish with fresh coriander if you like and serve.

in the
oven

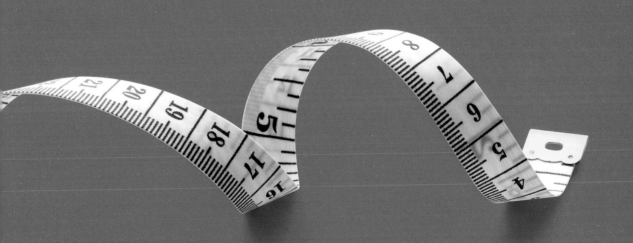

517
CALORIES
PER SERVING

roast chicken and savoury rice

SERVES 5

PREP: 15 MINUTES

COOK: 1½ HOURS

1.8kg whole chicken
juice and finely grated zest
   of 1 lemon
1 tbsp olive oil
4–5 sprigs of fresh thyme,
   leaves roughly chopped
   (about 2 tsp of leaves)
1 medium onion, finely
   chopped
1 red pepper, deseeded
   and cut into roughly
   1.5cm chunks
1 yellow pepper, deseeded
   and cut into roughly
   1.5cm chunks
2 garlic cloves, peeled
   and very thinly sliced
250g easy-cook, long
   grain rice
1 tsp ground turmeric
1 tsp ground cumin
1 tsp ground coriander
500ml hot chicken stock
   (made with 1 chicken
   stock cube)
flaked sea salt
ground black pepper
chopped fresh parsley,
   to garnish

A super way to roast chicken – this dish is served with savoury rice and lots of vegetables that make a nice change from potatoes. Serve with a large mixed salad drizzled with a mustardy balsamic vinaigrette (see below) and you won't need any gravy or sauce to accompany your bird.

Preheat the oven to 200°C/Fan 180°C/Gas 6. Place the chicken in a large, shallow ovenproof dish or roasting tin that holds 4 litres. Remove the trussing elastic and retie the chicken's legs with string if you like.

Rub the lemon juice over the chicken, then rub 1 teaspoon of the oil into the skin and sprinkle with the thyme and plenty of seasoning. Roast for 1 hour.

While the chicken is cooking, prepare the rice. Heat the remaining oil in a large non-stick frying pan and gently fry the onion and peppers for 5 minutes or until softened, stirring regularly. Stir in the garlic and spices, and cook for 1 minute more, adding a splash of water if they start to stick. Add the rice and stir well.

Take the chicken out of the oven and transfer to a board. Add the rice mixture to the tin and stir in the lemon zest and hot chicken stock. Place the chicken on top and cover the whole dish with a large piece of foil. Return to the oven and bake for a further 30 minutes, until the chicken is cooked throughout and the rice is tender. Take the chicken out of the dish and carve. Serve with the rice and a large mixed salad or green vegetables. Garnish with fresh parsley if you like.

Balsamic vinaigrette: Whisk 1 teaspoon of Dijon mustard with ½ crushed garlic clove, 2 tablespoons of thick balsamic vinegar, a good pinch of flaked sea salt and lots of ground black pepper. Slowly whisk in 3 tablespoons of olive oil until thickened and adjust the seasoning to taste. Serves 5. Calories per serving: 71

391

moroccan chicken tagine

1 tbsp sunflower oil
  or mild olive oil
2 medium onions, halved
  and thinly sliced
4 garlic cloves, peeled
  and thinly sliced
12 boneless, skinless
  chicken thighs (about
  1kg)
4 tsp ras-el-hanout
1 tsp cumin seeds
400ml hot chicken stock
  (made with 1 chicken
  stock cube)
2 x 400g cans chopped
  tomatoes
4 tsp harissa paste
  (from a jar)
2 tbsp clear honey
400g can chickpeas,
  drained and rinsed
400g sweet potatoes,
  peeled and cut into
  roughly 3cm chunks
75g dried giant couscous
15g bunch of fresh
  coriander, leaves
  chopped, plus extra
  to garnish
flaked sea salt
ground black pepper

Flat freeze the cooked and
cooled casserole in 2 large
freezer bags for up to
3 months. Thaw overnight in
the fridge. Reheat in a large
saucepan or flameproof
casserole with 200ml cold
water over a medium heat,
or in the microwave, stirring
until piping hot throughout.

This chicken tagine is a really convenient version using ready mixed spices and harissa paste. Giant couscous is simply larger balls of couscous made with durum wheat; just like pasta. Choose the wholegrain kind if you can – it cooks in the same time and has extra fibre. If you don't have ras-el-hanout, mix 2 teaspoons of ground coriander, 1½ teaspoons of ground cumin, 1 teaspoon of ground ginger and ½ teaspoon of ground cinnamon instead.

Heat the oil in a large flameproof casserole and fry the onions gently for 5 minutes until well softened and lightly browned, stirring regularly. Add the garlic and cook for 1 minute more, stirring.

While the onions and garlic are cooking, trim the excess fat from each chicken thigh – a set of kitchen scissors is good for this – and cut the thighs in half. Season all over with salt and pepper. Preheat the oven to 200°C/Fan 180°C/Gas 6.

Add the chicken to the onions and garlic, sprinkle with the ras-el-hanout and cumin and cook over a medium-high heat for 5–6 minutes or until lightly coloured all over, stirring and turning the chicken and onions regularly.

Pour over the chicken stock, then tip the tomatoes into the pan, add the harissa and honey and bring to a gentle simmer. Stir in the chickpeas and sweet potato. Cover with a lid and cook in the oven for 30 minutes.

Take the casserole out of the oven and stir in the couscous and coriander. Cover and return to the oven for a further 20 minutes or until the chicken is tender and the couscous is cooked. Sprinkle with a little more chopped coriander and serve with a lightly dressed green salad.

slow cooked beef ragu

SERVES 6

PREP: 20 MINUTES

COOK: 3½–4¼ HOURS

1 tbsp sunflower oil
2 medium onions, chopped
2 celery sticks, trimmed
   and thinly sliced
800kg braising beef
   (ideally chuck steak)
1 tsp flaked sea salt,
   plus extra to season
2 tsp dried mixed herbs
½ tsp dried chilli flakes
1 bay leaf
300ml red wine
3 x 400g cans chopped
   tomatoes
1 beef stock cube
1 tsp caster sugar
ground black pepper
chopped fresh parsley,
   to garnish

Flat freeze the cooked and cooled ragu in zip-seal bags for up to 3 months. Thaw overnight in the fridge and then reheat in the microwave or a large wide-based saucepan over a medium heat, stirring regularly until piping hot throughout.

Tip: If you are stuck for time, you can reheat the ragu from frozen. Place it in a large pan with a splash of water and warm through over a medium heat until piping hot. Stir regularly and don't worry if the meat falls apart a bit.

This is a wonderfully rich beef ragu that makes a lovely change from the classic Bolognese sauce when served with pasta. The long, slow cooking tenderises the meat and gives the tomatoes a sweet toasted flavour all their own. Buy good braising beef – the kind you need to cut yourself – rather than diced beef if you can.

Preheat the oven to 180°C/Fan 160°C/Gas 4. Heat the oil in a large flameproof casserole with a lid. Fry the onions and celery over a medium-high heat for 5 minutes until lightly browned, stirring regularly. Remove from the heat.

Meanwhile, trim the beef of any hard fat and sinew. Cut the beef into roughly 4cm chunks. Tip into the pan with the onions and cook together for a further 5–10 minutes or until the beef is lightly coloured all over.

Add the salt, herbs, chilli flakes, bay leaf, red wine, tomatoes and a few twists of freshly ground black pepper. Crumble the stock cube over, add the sugar, stir well and bring to a simmer.

Cover the casserole with a lid and carefully transfer it to the oven. Cook for 3½–4 hours or until the beef is very tender and the sauce is thick, stirring every hour if you can. Garnish with fresh parsley just before seving if you like.

Buttered tagliatelle: Cook 300g dried egg tagliatelle in boiling water for about 8 minutes or according to the packet instructions, stirring occasionally. Drain in a colander and return to the saucepan. Toss with 15g butter and salt and pepper to taste. Serves 6. Calories per serving: 190

354
CALORIES
PER SERVING

spaghetti pie

SERVES 6

PREP: 25 MINUTES

COOK: 1¼ HOURS

450g lean minced beef
(10% fat or less)
1 medium onion, finely
chopped
2 garlic cloves, crushed
1 tsp dried oregano
1 tsp dried mint
½ tsp dried rosemary
100ml red wine or extra
beef stock
500ml beef stock (made
with 1 beef stock cube)
400g can chopped
tomatoes
2 tbsp tomato purée
2 medium courgettes, cut
into roughly 1cm slices
150g long macaroni or
bucatini pasta
200g young spinach leaves,
rinsed in cold water
50g Parmesan cheese,
finely grated
flaked sea salt
ground black pepper

FOR THE WHITE SAUCE
450ml semi-skimmed milk
3 tbsp cornflour
(about 30g)
2 bay leaves
¼ tsp ground nutmeg
flaked sea salt
ground black pepper

Tip: You can use lamb mince
and stock instead of beef but
you'll need to add an extra
55 calories per serving.

A Greek version of lasagne made with long macaroni instead of
sheets of pasta. Use thick spaghetti if you can't find the kind with
a hole through the centre. Serve with a large mixed salad.

Put the beef, onion, garlic, oregano, mint and rosemary in a
large non-stick saucepan or sauté pan and cook over a medium
heat for 10 minutes, stirring and squashing with a wooden
spoon to break up the meat.

Season with salt and plenty of freshly ground black pepper. Pour
over the wine, if using, and add the stock, tomatoes and tomato
purée. Bring to a gentle simmer and cook for 30 minutes, stirring
occasionally. Add the courgettes and cook for 10 minutes more or
until the beef is tender and the sauce is thick, stirring occasionally.

While the mince is simmering, half fill a large saucepan
with water and bring it to the boil. Add the pasta and cook
for about 10 minutes, stirring occasionally until nearly cooked.
Drain in a colander then return to the saucepan and toss with
the spinach. Cook over a low heat for 2 minutes or until the
spinach softens. Season with lots of ground black pepper
and set aside.

Preheat the oven to 200°C/Fan 180°C/Gas 6. Just before the
mince is ready, make the white sauce. Mix 4 tablespoons of
the milk with the cornflour in a small bowl until smooth. Put
to one side. Pour the rest of the milk into a medium non-stick
saucepan and add the bay leaves. Heat gently for 5 minutes
or until almost at a simmer, stirring regularly.

Remove the bay leaves and whisk in the cornflour mixture
with a silicone-covered whisk. Cook over a medium heat
until thickened, stirring with the whisk until smooth. Remove
from the heat. Season with the nutmeg, salt and black pepper.

Pour half the mince mixture into a 3 litre ovenproof dish and
top with half the pasta; repeat the layers ending with the pasta.
Pour over the white sauce, so it mostly covers the pasta,
sprinkle with the cheese and bake for 20 minutes or until
golden brown and bubbling.

186
CALORIES
PER HALF PEPPER

hungarian turkey stuffed peppers

SERVES 6

PREP: 25 MINUTES

COOK: 1 HOUR

75g easy-cook, long
  grain rice
3 large red peppers
1 tbsp sunflower oil
1 medium onion, finely
  chopped
1 medium courgette, cut
  into roughly 1.5cm chunks
3 garlic cloves, crushed
1 tsp hot smoked paprika
3 tsp paprika (not smoked),
  plus extra to sprinkle
2 tsp flaked sea salt
250g turkey breast mince
  (about 2% fat)
15g fresh parsley, leaves
  finely chopped
15g fresh dill, leaves finely
  chopped, plus extra
  to garnish
100g soured cream, to
  serve
ground black pepper

Tip: Any leftover turkey
mince can be flat frozen
in a freezer bag for up
to 3 months.

Eastern Europe has many stuffed vegetable dishes and I've used lots of ingredients that are popular in Hungary, so these peppers have a Hungarian twist. Serve half a pepper for a light lunch or both halves for a more substantial meal. Any leftover peppers will be delicious served cold with a salad.

To make the stuffing, half fill a medium saucepan with water and bring it to the boil. Add the rice and cook for 10 minutes. Rinse the cooked rice in a sieve under running water until cold. Drain and place in the fridge.

Preheat the oven to 200°C/Fan 180°C/Gas 6. Cut the peppers in half from stem to base and carefully remove the seeds. Place the peppers, cut side up, in a shallow ovenproof dish or roasting tin. (Cut a thin sliver off the base of any peppers that don't sit flat.) Set aside.

Pour the oil into a large non-stick saucepan and fry the onion and courgette over a medium heat for 3 minutes, stirring until beginning to brown. Add the garlic and cook for 1 minute more, stirring.

Reduce the heat to low and stir in both types of paprika, the salt and lots of ground black pepper. Cook for a further minute, stirring continuously, then remove from the heat and tip the mixture into a heatproof bowl.

Add the rice, turkey mince, chopped parsley, dill and lots of seasoning, then mix until thoroughly combined. (If making ahead, leave the onion and courgette to cool completely before mixing them with the turkey and rice.) Season to taste. Spoon the stuffing mixture loosely into the peppers; don't press down hard or the filling will compact.

Cover the dish with foil and bake for 45 minutes or until the peppers are tender and the turkey is hot and cooked through. Remove the foil for the last 15 minutes. Serve with spoonfuls of soured cream and roughly chopped fresh dill alongside a large mixed salad.

508
CALORIES
PER SERVING

tuscan pork ragu

SERVES 6
PREP: 20 MINUTES
COOK: 3¼ HOURS

1 tbsp sunflower oil
2 medium red onions, chopped
2 celery sticks, trimmed and thinly sliced
6 garlic cloves, peeled and crushed
1kg shoulder of pork
1 tsp flaked sea salt, plus extra to season
2 tsp dried oregano
½ tsp dried chilli flakes
2 bay leaves
300ml red wine
2 x 400g cans chopped tomatoes
100g pitted black olives, drained
3 tbsp capers, drained
3 tbsp thick balsamic vinegar
300g dried pappardelle pasta
roughly chopped flat-leaf parsley, to garnish
ground black pepper

Freeze the cooked and cooled ragu in freezer-proof containers for up to 3 months. Thaw overnight in the fridge. Reheat in a large wide-based saucepan or flameproof casserole with 200ml cold water over a medium heat, or in the microwave, stirring occasionally until piping hot throughout.

Shoulder of pork is an inexpensive cut that is delicious when simmered slowly with tomatoes, chilli, herbs, olives and capers – plus plenty of red wine. Serve with wide pappardelle pasta or tagliatelle if you prefer. (It's really good with mashed potatoes too!)

Preheat the oven to 180°C/Fan 160°C/Gas 4. Heat the oil in a large flameproof casserole with a lid. Fry the onions and celery over a medium-high heat for about 10 minutes until lightly browned, stirring regularly. Add the garlic and cook for 1 minute more. Remove from the heat.

Meanwhile, trim the pork of any rind and obvious fat. Cut the meat into roughly 4cm chunks. Tip the chunks into the casserole with the onions and fry together for 5 minutes, stirring regularly.

Add the salt, oregano, chilli flakes, bay leaves, red wine, tomatoes, olives, capers, balsamic vinegar and a few twists of freshly ground black pepper. Stir well and bring to the boil.

Cover the casserole with a lid and carefully transfer to the oven. Cook for 3 hours or until the pork is very tender and the sauce is thick. Stir every hour if you can, but it's not essential.

Ten minutes before the pork is ready, half fill a large saucepan with water and bring it to the boil. Add the pasta, return to the boil and cook for about 10 minutes or according to the packet instructions until tender, stirring occasionally. Drain in a colander.

Serve the hot ragu with the freshly cooked pasta and a lightly dressed green salad, garnished with the chopped parsley.

191

baked tomatoes with spiced lamb

MAKES 6

PREP: 25 MINUTES

COOK: 55 MINUTES

1 small onion, finely chopped

1 medium courgette, cut into roughly 1.5cm chunks

1 small red pepper, deseeded and cut into roughly 1.5cm chunks

250g minced lamb (10% fat or less)

1 tbsp medium curry powder

1 tsp ground cumin

1 tsp ground turmeric

2 garlic cloves, crushed

175ml lamb stock (made with ½ lamb stock cube)

6 beef tomatoes (each about 300g)

250g sachet steamed brown basmati rice

25g sultanas

10g flaked almonds

15g bunch of fresh coriander, leaves finely chopped

flaked sea salt

ground black pepper

Tip: Beef tomatoes are sometimes called slicing tomatoes in the supermarket.

If you aren't confident about cooking rice – especially brown rice – this is the recipe for you. I've used a sachet of cooked steamed brown basmati rice, available from larger supermarkets, as the base for my spiced lamb filling. There's no need to serve anything else except a large salad as everything is contained within the tomatoes.

Place a large non-stick saucepan over a medium-low heat. Dry fry the onion, courgette, pepper and lamb for 6–8 minutes, stirring regularly and squashing the meat with a wooden spoon until it is beginning to brown.

Add the spices and garlic and fry for 1 minute more, stirring. Stir in the stock and bring to a simmer. Cook for 15 minutes, stirring occasionally until the liquid is absorbed.

Meanwhile, preheat the oven to 220°C/Fan 200°C/Gas 7. Slice the tops off the tomatoes and reserve. Carefully scoop out the seeds and pulp into a bowl with a teaspoon.

Remove the saucepan from the heat and stir in the rice, 3 tablespoons of the tomato juice, the sultanas, almonds, coriander and salt and pepper to taste. Cook for 1–2 minutes, stirring, until the rice is hot.

Place the scooped out tomatoes in a shallow baking dish or roasting tin and fill them with the rice mixture. Replace the tops. Bake for 20–25 minutes until the filling is hot throughout and the tomatoes are softened and lightly browned.

322
CALORIES
PER SERVING

chinese-style sea bass

SERVES 4
PREP: 15 MINUTES
COOK: 20 MINUTES

2 medium carrots (each about 100g), peeled
1 red pepper, deseeded
4 spring onions, trimmed
20g chunk of fresh root ginger, peeled
2 tsp sunflower oil, plus extra for greasing
2 large garlic cloves, thinly sliced
100g sugar snap peas, trimmed and halved lengthways
4 sea bass fillets or sea bream fillets (each about 125g)
½ tsp Chinese five-spice powder
250g sachet steamed basmati rice
ground black pepper

FOR THE DRESSING
3 tbsp fresh lime juice
1½ tbsp Thai fish sauce (nam pla)
2 tsp toasted sesame oil
2 tbsp soft light brown sugar
½ tsp dried chilli flakes

Tip: You'll need about 1½ limes to get 3 tablespoons of fresh juice, depending on how large and juicy they are.

Pre-steamed basmati rice is a great store-cupboard favourite of mine. It comes in sachets and is very useful when I want to knock up a quick stuffing such as the one used for this Chinese-style sea bass.

Cut the carrots, pepper, spring onions and ginger into julienne strips, first cutting them into short lengths and then slicing them into slender matchsticks. Heat the oil in a large wok or sauté pan over a high heat. Stir-fry the carrots, pepper, spring onions, ginger, garlic and sugar snap peas for 1 minute. Tip everything into a large bowl.

Pat the sea bass fillets dry and slash the skin of each fillet 3–4 times with a sharp knife. Sprinkle the flesh of each fillet with a little five-spice powder and rub in well. Preheat the oven to 220°C/Fan 200°C/Gas 7.

When ready to assemble, stir the rice into the vegetable mixture then place the mixture in heaps on a large, lightly greased baking tray. Spread until the piles are roughly the same size as a fish fillet. Place the fish on top of the rice mixture and season with some black pepper.

Bake for 12–15 minutes or until the fish is just cooked and the filling is hot. This will depend on the thickness of your fillets. While the fish is cooking, mix all the ingredients for the dressing together in a small bowl.

Divide the fish and vegetables carefully between 4 warmed plates and spoon over a little of the dressing to serve.

ricotta and spinach pasta parcels

SERVES 4

PREP: 25 MINUTES

COOK: 30 MINUTES

6 fresh lasagne sheets
(each about 35g),
cut in half widthways
350g tomato and basil
pasta sauce (from a jar)
25g Parmesan cheese,
finely grated
1 tsp pumpkin seeds
(optional)
basil leaves, to garnish
(optional)

FOR THE FILLING

1 tbsp mild olive oil or
sunflower oil, plus extra
for greasing
1 medium onion, peeled,
sliced and finely chopped
250g young spinach leaves
2 garlic cloves, peeled
and crushed
1 large egg
250g pot of ricotta cheese
2 tsp cornflour
½ tsp freshly grated
or ground nutmeg
½ tsp fine sea salt
ground black pepper

Tip: If you don't want to use
fresh lasagne sheets, boil
8 dried sheets until tender
then rinse in cold water and
cut in half. Fill as above.

This pasta bake is a doddle to make and looks pretty impressive when taken to the table. I cut corners by using a ready-made pasta sauce for the topping – they tend to be fairly low in calories, so choose your favourite brand.

To make the filling, heat the oil in a large saucepan and gently fry the onion for 5 minutes or until softened, stirring regularly. Add the spinach and garlic and cook over a medium-high heat to drive off most of the water and soften the leaves.

Tip the spinach mixture into a sieve over a bowl and press firmly with a ladle or wooden spoon to remove as much moisture as possible.

Meanwhile, half fill a heatproof bowl with just-boiled water from the kettle and add the lasagne sheets, one at a time. Leave to soak.

Beat the egg in a large bowl with a metal whisk, then add the ricotta, cornflour, nutmeg, salt and lots of ground black pepper. Preheat the oven to 200°C/Fan 180°C/Gas 6. Lightly oil a 2 litre shallow ovenproof dish (a lasagne dish is ideal).

Drain the lasagne. Take one halved sheet and spoon the ricotta mixture down the centre, from one corner to the other. Fold it over into a loose triangle to enclose the filling and place in the dish. It doesn't matter if the filling isn't completely enclosed. Repeat the process until all the lasagne and the filling has been used.

Pour the tomato sauce over the pasta, sprinkle with Parmesan and the pumpkin seeds, if using, and bake for 25 minutes or until piping hot throughout and golden brown and bubbling. Garnish with fresh basil leaves and serve with a large mixed salad if you like.

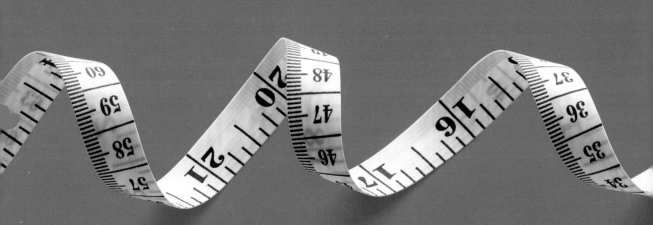

something
new

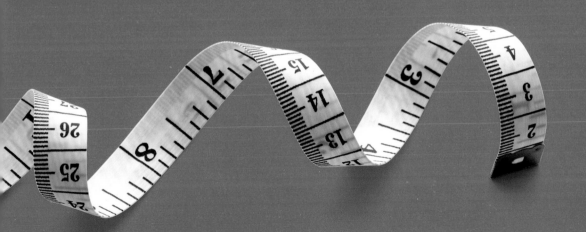

314
CALORIES
PER SERVING

chicken pho

SERVES 4
PREP: 20 MINUTES
COOK: 1 HOUR

2 medium onions, peeled
   and cut into 6 wedges
4 garlic cloves, peeled and
   thinly sliced
25g chunk of fresh root
   ginger, peeled and
   thinly sliced
4 red bird's eye chillies, cut
   in half lengthways
   (deseed first if you like),
   or 1 tsp dried chilli flakes
1 tsp Chinese five-spice
   powder
1.3 litres cold water
4 tbsp dark soy sauce,
   plus extra to serve
2 tbsp Thai fish sauce
   (nam pla)
1 small chicken (about
   1.2kg), skin removed
flaked sea salt
ground black pepper

FOR THE VEGETABLES
200g dried flat rice noodles
½ tsp sunflower oil
300g long stemmed
   broccoli, trimmed
6 spring onions, thinly sliced
200g bean sprouts, rinsed
   and drained
25g bunch of fresh coriander
2 red bird's eye chillies,
   thinly sliced
lime wedges, for squeezing

Tip: Remove the chicken
skin by pushing your fingers
between the skin and flesh,
easing off the skin. Snip off
when you reach the wing
tips and legs.

This is my simplified version of chicken pho, a Vietnamese
dish of noodles in a richly flavoured stock. If you don't use all
the cooked chicken in your pho, chill it in the fridge and use
it for sandwiches or a salad the next day.

Preheat the oven to 200°C/Fan 180°C/Gas 6. Put the onions,
garlic, ginger, chillies and five-spice powder in a flameproof
casserole. Stir in the water, soy sauce and fish sauce.

Place the chicken, breast-side up, in the spiced stock and
season with a little salt and lots of ground black pepper. Bring
the water to a very gentle simmer and cover the casserole with a
lid. Place in the oven for 50 minutes or until the chicken is
thoroughly cooked and very tender.

Just before the chicken is ready, put the noodles in a saucepan
or large heatproof bowl and cover with just-boiled water.
Leave to stand for about 10 minutes, or according to the packet
instructions, until just tender, stirring regularly to separate the
strands. Drain in a sieve under running water until cold, toss
with the oil and set aside.

Transfer the chicken to a board and strip off the meat in large
pieces, discarding the bones. Slice the chicken thickly. Cover
with foil to keep warm. Strain the stock from the casserole
through a sieve into a large saucepan. Discard the onions,
garlic, ginger and chillies. Skim off the fat from the stock with
a large spoon and bring to a gentle simmer. Add the broccoli
and cook for 3 minutes or until just tender. Add the noodles
and warm through in the hot stock.

Divide the noodles and broccoli between 4 large deep bowls.
Place the chicken on top and arrange the spring onions, bean
sprouts and coriander in piles near the chicken. Ladle over
the hot stock and serve with extra soy sauce, the sliced
chillies and lime wedges for squeezing over.

499
CALORIES
PER SERVING

royal chicken korma with coriander rice

SERVES 4

**PREP: 25 MINUTES,
PLUS MARINATING TIME**

COOK: 30–35 MINUTES

4 boneless, skinless chicken
   breasts (each about 150g)
100g fat-free natural
   yoghurt
2 tbsp medium curry
   powder
1 tbsp sunflower oil
2 medium onions, thinly
   sliced
2 tbsp ground almonds
2 tsp caster sugar
1 tsp flaked sea salt,
   plus extra to season
¼ tsp ground cinnamon
250ml cold water
2 tsp dried fenugreek
   leaves (methi)
3 tbsp double cream
200g basmati rice
25g bunch of fresh
   coriander, leaves finely
   chopped, plus sprigs
   to garnish
ground black pepper
15g toasted flaked almonds,
   to serve

Freeze the cooked and
cooled curry in freezer bags
for up to 4 months. Defrost
in the fridge overnight and
reheat thoroughly in a large
saucepan or the microwave,
stirring regularly until
piping hot throughout.

Dried fenugreek (methi) is the secret ingredient for this
chicken curry. You can find it in the Indian section of larger
supermarkets. If you can't find any, add three tablespoons of
finely chopped coriander or fresh fenugreek leaves instead.

Trim the chicken breasts, remove any visible fat with kitchen
scissors, and cut each into 9 even pieces. Put them in a bowl
and add the yoghurt and 1 tablespoon of curry powder. Stir well,
cover and marinate in the fridge for 3–4 hours or overnight.

To make the sauce, heat the oil in a large non-stick saucepan or
sauté pan over a low heat. Add the onions, cover with a lid and
fry gently for 10 minutes or until softened. Stir the onions every
so often so they don't stick to the pan. After 10 minutes, remove
the lid, turn up the heat and fry for 5 minutes more or until lightly
browned, stirring regularly. Add the remaining curry powder
and cook for 1 minute. Stir in the sugar, salt, cinnamon and water.
Bring to the boil and cook for 2 minutes.

Take the pan off the heat and blitz the onions with a stick
blender until as smooth as possible. (Alternatively, let the
onions cool for a few minutes and blend them in a food
processor before returning them to the pan.)

Return the saucepan to the heat and add the ground almonds
and water. Sprinkle the fenugreek leaves on top, stir and bring
to a gentle simmer.

Add the chicken and marinade to the pan. Simmer for 10–12
minutes or until the sauce is thick and the chicken is cooked
through, stirring regularly. Stir in the cream and season with
salt and pepper to taste.

While the chicken is simmering, cook the rice. Half fill a large
pan with water and bring to the boil. Rinse the rice in a sieve
under cold water for a few seconds then add to the hot water.
Stir well and return to the boil. Cook for about 10 minutes or
according to the packet instructions, stirring occasionally until
tender. Drain and return to the pan. Toss with the coriander and
serve with the curry, sprinkled with flaked almonds.

466

jerk chicken with rice and beans

SERVES 6
**PREP: 35 MINUTES,
PLUS MARINATING TIME**
COOK: 35 MINUTES

12 boneless, skinless
   chicken thighs (about
   1kg)
50g desiccated coconut
½ tsp ground turmeric
400ml just-boiled water
oil, for brushing or spraying
250g easy-cook, long
   grain rice
400g can red kidney beans,
   rinsed and drained
4 spring onions, trimmed
   and thinly sliced
flaked sea salt
ground black pepper
lime wedges, to serve
fresh thyme or coriander,
   to garnish (optional)

FOR THE MARINADE
4 spring onions, trimmed
   and roughly chopped
20g chunk of fresh root
   ginger, peeled and
   roughly chopped
4 garlic cloves, peeled
   and halved
2–3 scotch bonnet chillies
   (the more you use
   the hotter it will be),
   stalks removed
1 tbsp fresh thyme leaves
   (or 1 tsp dried thyme)
1 tsp ground allspice
½ tsp ground nutmeg
½ tsp ground cinnamon
3 tbsp dark brown sugar
2 tbsp fresh lime juice
   (from 1 large lime)
1½ tbsp dark soy sauce

If you can't get hold of scotch bonnet chillies, use two red bird's eye chillies and two plump red chillies instead. But don't deseed them – you need the heat for this marinade. I give the rice a mild coconut flavour without using high-fat coconut milk by soaking desiccated coconut in hot water.

To make the marinade, put all the ingredients in a food processor and blitz to a thick purée. You will need to remove the lid and push the mixture down a couple of times with a rubber spatula until the right consistency is reached.

Put the chicken on a board and trim off as much fat as possible with a set of kitchen scissors. Slash each thigh a couple of times with a sharp knife, then put them in a bowl. Pour the jerk marinade over and mix well. Cover and chill for at least 2 hours or overnight.

Put the coconut in a large heatproof bowl with the turmeric and pour over the just-boiled water. Leave to stand for 2 hours or overnight.

Preheat the oven to 220°C/Fan 200°C/Gas 7. Place the chicken in a lightly oiled roasting tin, shaking off any excess marinade as you go. Form the chicken pieces into neat thigh shapes. Brush or spray with a little oil and bake them for 20 minutes.

Stir the rice, kidney beans and spring onions into the coconut and turmeric water. Take the roasting tin out of the oven and spoon the rice around the chicken pieces. Cover the tin with a large piece of foil and bake for 15 minutes or until the rice is tender and has absorbed all the liquid and the chicken is thoroughly cooked. Serve hot or cold with a large mixed salad and lime wedges for squeezing. Garnish with fresh thyme or coriander if you like.

377
CALORIES
PER SERVING

pad thai

150g flat dried rice noodles
1 tsp sunflower oil, plus
    1 tbsp
2½ tbsp Thai fish sauce
    (nam pla), plus extra
    to season
juice of 1 large lime
    (about 2 tbsp)
1 tbsp light soft brown
    sugar
4 boneless, skinless chicken
    thighs
1 medium red onion,
    cut into 12 wedges
2 garlic cloves, finely
    chopped
½ tsp dried chilli flakes
2 medium eggs, well beaten
100g cooked and peeled
    cold water prawns,
    thawed if frozen
20g roasted salted peanuts,
    roughly chopped
8 spring onions, trimmed
    and sliced
100g bean sprouts, rinsed
    and drained
15g bunch of fresh
    coriander, leaves
    roughly chopped
soy sauce, to season

Make sure you have everything ready before you begin to cook as this dish is very quick to make once all the preparation is done.

Half fill a large saucepan with water and bring it to the boil. Add the noodles, turn off the heat and leave to stand for about 5–10 minutes, or according to the packet instructions, until tender. Stir with a fork every couple of minutes to separate the strands.

Drain the noodles in a colander and toss with the teaspoon of oil to stop them sticking together, then put to one side. Mix the fish sauce, lime juice and sugar in a small bowl. Trim any visible fat off the chicken thighs and cut each one into 6 pieces.

Pour the remaining tablespoon of oil into a large wok or non-stick frying pan and stir-fry the red onion and chicken over a medium heat for 2 minutes. Add the garlic and chilli flakes and cook for 30 seconds more. Push all the vegetables and chicken to one side of the pan.

Pour the beaten eggs into the pan and allow them to cook into a thin omelette on the bottom. This should take 30–40 seconds. Just before the egg is completely set, use a wooden spoon to roughly chop it.

Immediately add the prawns, soaked noodles, peanuts, spring onions and fish sauce mixture. Increase the heat to its highest setting and stir-fry together for 2 minutes. Toss all the ingredients with tongs or 2 wooden spoons as you stir-fry to make sure everything is thoroughly hot and well mixed.

Add the bean sprouts and coriander and stir-fry for 2–3 minutes more or until the noodles and eggs are lightly browned in places. Divide the pad Thai between warmed plates or bowls using tongs. Serve with extra fish sauce and soy sauce for seasoning.

126

hoisin pork rolls

MAKES 8

**PREP: 20 MINUTES,
PLUS COOLING TIME**

COOK: 6 MINUTES

1 tsp sunflower oil
250g lean pork mince
 (8% fat or less)
6 spring onions, trimmed
 and thinly sliced
3 tbsp hoisin sauce (from a
 jar or bottle)
8 spring roll wrappers
 (made from rice)
20g bunch of coriander,
 trimmed
1 medium carrot (about
 100g), peeled and grated
 into long strips
1 romaine lettuce heart,
 or 2 little gem lettuces,
 leaves shredded

FOR THE DIPPING SAUCE
3 tbsp Thai sweet chilli
 dipping sauce
2 tbsp cold water

Tip: Coarsley grate the
carrot carefully in an
upright position so the
strips will be longer and
more elegant.

These pork rolls make a fresh light meal and are perfect served cold on a warm day. The rice wrappers are sold as clear hard sheets that look like plastic – you'll find them in the pasta and rice section at larger supermarkets or Asian shops. When soaked in water they become soft and pliable, almost translucent and ready-to-eat.

Heat the oil in a non-stick frying pan or wok and stir-fry the pork for 5 minutes, using 2 wooden spoons to squash the meat against the side of the pan to break it up. Add the spring onions and hoisin sauce and cook for 1 minute more or until the pork is cooked through and there is no pink remaining. Tip everything onto a plate and leave to cool for 30 minutes.

Boil a kettle of water, then pour the water into a heatproof bowl. Leave the water to cool for 5 minutes. Take a spring roll wrapper and use tongs to dip it into the water. Remove it immediately and place it on a board.

Spoon a few coriander leaves down the centre of the wrapper and top with an eighth of the pork mixture. Place a mixture of the coriander, lettuce and carrot on top of the pork.

Bring the bottom end of the wrapper up over the filling and then the other, followed by both sides. Place the roll on a plate with the fold-side down. Repeat with the remaining wrappers until all the filling is used up. Make a quick dipping sauce for the rolls by mixing Thai sweet chilli sauce with water. Keep the rolls and sauce in the fridge until ready to serve.

302
CALORIES
PER SERVING

singapore noodles

SERVES 4

PREP: 15 MINUTES

COOK: 30 MINUTES

3 tbsp hoisin sauce (from a
   jar or bottle)
275g pork tenderloin (fillet),
   trimmed of fat and sinew
100g dried fine egg noodles
1 tbsp sunflower oil
1 medium red onion,
   cut into thin wedges
1 red pepper, deseeded
   and thinly sliced
150g shiitake mushrooms,
   thickly sliced
2 garlic cloves, crushed
20g fresh root ginger,
   peeled and finely grated
2 tsp medium curry powder
150g cooked and peeled
   cold water prawns,
   thawed if frozen
50g frozen peas
2 tbsp dark soy sauce

A filling and comforting supper dish with a fusion of Indian and Asian flavours. This is a great one for relaxed family eating but make sure you have roasted your pork and prepared the other ingredients before you stir-fry as it's very quick once you start.

Preheat the oven to 200°C/Fan 180°C/Gas 6. Put the hoisin sauce in a bowl and add the pork. Turn several times until it is well coated with the sauce.

Place the pork on a foil-lined baking tray. Roast for 20 minutes or until it is cooked through, sticky and glossy. Remove from the oven and leave to stand.

While the pork is cooking, put the noodles in a large bowl and cover with just-boiled water. Leave to stand for 3 minutes, or according to the packet instructions, then drain well in a sieve. Rinse under running water until cold then drain.

Place a large non-stick frying pan or wok over a medium heat. Add the oil and stir-fry the onion, red pepper and mushrooms for 5 minutes or until they begin to soften and lightly colour. Stir in the garlic and ginger and stir-fry for 1 minute. Sprinkle the curry powder into the pan and cook for 30 seconds, stirring continuously. (Add a splash of water if the spice starts to stick).

Thinly slice the pork and add to the hot pan along with the prawns and peas. Stir-fry for 1 minute then add the drained noodles and soy sauce. Toss together for 2–3 minutes or until piping hot throughout. Serve immediately.

69

CALORIES
PER ROLL

crab sushi rolls

MAKES 12

PREP: 30 MINUTES,
PLUS COOLING TIME

COOK: 30 MINUTES

300ml cold water
200g sushi rice
1½ tbsp rice vinegar
1½ tsp caster sugar
1½ tsp fine sea salt
1 tbsp reduced-fat (light)
  mayonnaise
120g cooked white
  crabmeat, from a tub
  or can, drained
2 sushi nori sheets
  (dried seaweed)
½ small red pepper,
  deseeded and cut
  into very thin strips
6cm length of cucumber,
  seeds removed, cut into
  5mm-wide batons

TO SERVE (OPTIONAL)
pickled ginger, drained
dark soy sauce mixed
  with chilli flakes
wasabi paste

Tip: Use canned tuna or
finely chopped cooked
and peeled prawns instead
of the crab if you prefer.

My sushi rolls are larger than normal, so less of a fiddle
to prepare. I've filled them with a mixture of cooked crab,
cucumber and pepper. Serve with pickled ginger and dark soy
sauce for dipping. If you haven't tried making maki sushi before,
be brave and give it a go – these really couldn't be easier.

Bring the water to the boil in a small saucepan. Add the rice
and return to the boil. Cover with a tight-fitting lid and turn
down the heat to a very low simmer. Cook for 20 minutes.

Remove the pan from the heat and leave to stand for 10 minutes.
While the rice is standing, mix the vinegar, sugar and salt
together in a small non-metallic bowl.

When the rice is ready, pour the vinegar mixture over it and stir
well. Tip the rice onto a large plate and spread it out into a thin
layer. Cover and leave to cool in the fridge for about 30 minutes
or until completely cold.

Mix the mayonnaise and crab together in a bowl. Lay a sheet
of nori shiny side down on a clean board. Spread half the
rice over three-quarters of the nori, leaving a 5cm gap at the
end furthest away from you, and smooth it out with the back
of a dessertspoon. Take the spoon, or a damp finger, and
press it horizontally along the middle of the rice to create
a shallow groove.

Spoon half the crabmeat down the groove and top with the
pepper and cucumber strips, all facing the same direction.
Dab the uncovered nori with a little water, take the side closest
to you and start rolling using both hands to make a fat roll.
Roll it firmly so the filling stays together when the rolls are cut.

Trim the ends to neaten them, then cut the roll into slices.
Repeat with the other sheet of nori and filling ingredients.
Stand for about 10 minutes to allow the nori to soften and
then serve with pickled ginger, soy sauce and wasabi if you like.
Chill if not serving immediately.

53

salmon and avocado nigiri sushi

MAKES 12
PREP: 10 MINUTES,
PLUS COOLING TIME
COOK: 30 MINUTES

700ml cold water
125g sushi rice, well rinsed
in cold water
1½ tbsp rice vinegar,
plus 2 tbsp for forming
the nigiri
1 tsp caster sugar
1 tsp flaked sea salt
½ small ripe avocado
1 tbsp reduced-fat (light)
mayonnaise
40g sliced smoked salmon,
cut into roughly 5 x 2cm
rectangles
1 strip of nori (dried
seaweed), about 2cm
wide (optional)
wasabi paste and pickled
ginger, to serve (optional)

FOR THE DIPPING SAUCE
3 tbsp dark soy sauce
½ tsp dried chilli flakes
¼ tsp sesame seeds
sliced red chilli (optional)

Tip: You'll find sushi rice,
wasabi and nori in the
Japanese section of the
supermarket, in Asian food
stores and online. You'll
need to mix wasabi powder
with a little water before
using it. You don't have to
wrap each piece with nori
but it makes them look
more authentic.

This recipe uses one of my favourite combinations – salmon and
avocado, both full of healthy oils. If you've never made sushi
before, these are a great place to start as there is no rolling
involved.

To prepare the rice, bring 200ml of the water to the boil in
a small saucepan. Add the rice and return to the boil. Cover
with a lid, reduce the heat to very low and cook for 20 minutes.

Remove the pan from the heat, keeping the lid on, and leave
to stand for 10 minutes. This will allow the rice to absorb the
rest of the water and continue cooking without breaking up.

Meanwhile, mix 1 tablespoon of the vinegar, the sugar and salt
together in a small bowl until the sugar has dissolved. Stir the
vinegar solution into the rice until it coats every grain. Tip the rice
onto a large plate and spread it out into a thin layer. Cover and
leave to cool in the fridge for 30 minutes or until completely cold.

Remove the avocado stone and scoop the flesh onto a board
using a large spoon. Finely dice the avocado and put it in
a bowl. Add the mayonnaise and stir until combined.

Mix the remaining vinegar with the remaining 500ml of cold
water in a large bowl. Dip your palms into the water. Pick up
a ball of rice (about 20g) and use your hands to shape it into
a small rectangle, roughly 5cm long, 3cm high and 2cm wide.
Put it on a small board or platter. Continue with the remaining
rice until you have made 12 evenly sized rectangles.

Spread a teaspoonful of the avocado mixture down the centre
of each rectangle. Cut the salmon into 12 neat rectangles the
same size as the rice rectangles and drape them over the rice.

Cut the nori into 12 strips 3mm wide and wrap around each
piece of sushi. Chill until required and eat the same day as they
are made. Mix the ingredients for the dipping sauce in a small
bowl. Serve the sushi with the sauce, wasabi paste and pickled
ginger if you like.

64
CALORIES
PER CAKE

salmon, rice and coriander cakes with tomato chilli jam

MAKES 12
PREP: 20 MINUTES
COOK: 15 MINUTES

2 x 125g fresh salmon
   fillets, skinned
2 garlic cloves, peeled
   and finely grated
1 tbsp harissa paste
   (from a jar)
2 tsp ras-el-hanout
finely grated zest of
   ½ lemon or 1 lime
1 tsp flaked sea salt
250g sachet pre-cooked
   long grain rice
4 spring onions, trimmed
   and finely sliced
15g bunch of fresh
   coriander, leaves finely
   chopped, plus extra
   to garnish
oil, for brushing or spraying
ground black pepper
lime or lemon wedges,
   for squeezing

These fishcakes make a healthy meal or snack and they are a nice change from fishcakes made with mashed potatoes. They can be eaten hot or cold and I serve mine with fresh tomato and chilli jam (see below) and a green leafy salad.

Preheat the oven to 200°C/Fan 180°C/Gas 6. Put the fish fillets, garlic, harissa, ras-el-hanout, lemon or lime zest, salt and a good grinding of black pepper in a food processor and blend to a thick paste. You may need to remove the lid and push the mixture down a couple of times with a spatula until the right consistency is reached.

Add the rice, spring onions and coriander and blend a couple of times on the pulse setting until just mixed. Remove the blade and with wet hands, form the mixture into 12 small balls, then flatten them into fishcakes about 1.5cm thick. (Wetting your hands in cold water should stop the salmon mixture sticking to them.)

Place the fishcakes on a lightly greased baking tray and bake for 15 minutes, turning them after 10 minutes. Serve the hot fishcakes with tomato jam and lime or lemon wedges for squeezing. Garnish with fresh coriander if you like.

Tomato and chilli jam: Put 350g roughly chopped fresh ripe tomatoes, 1 finely chopped long red chilli (deseed first if you like), 4 crushed garlic cloves, 1 tablespoon finely grated fresh root ginger, 75g demerara sugar and 75ml red wine vinegar in a medium non-stick saucepan and bring to a gentle simmer. Cover loosely with a lid and cook for 40 minutes, stirring occasionally until thick and glossy. Leave to cool before serving. (If covered in the fridge, this relish will keep for at least a week.) Serves 6. Calories per serving: 65

400

CALORIES
PER SERVING

simple spanish paella

SERVES 6
PREP: 25 MINUTES
COOK: 40 MINUTES

good pinch of saffron
   threads
650ml just-boiled water
1 chicken stock cube
6 boneless, skinless chicken
   thighs (about 500g)
1 tbsp olive oil
1 medium onion,
   finely chopped
1 red pepper, deseeded
   and cut into roughly
   3cm chunks
1 green pepper, deseeded
   and cut into roughly
   3cm chunks
1 yellow pepper, deseeded
   and cut into roughly
   3cm chunks
75g chorizo, skinned and
   cut into 5mm slices
250g Arborio (risotto) rice
1 tsp hot smoked paprika
1kg fresh live mussels
250g cooked and peeled
   cold water prawns,
   thawed if frozen
15g bunch of fresh flat-leaf
   parsley, leaves roughly
   chopped, plus extra
   to garnish
flaked sea salt
ground black pepper
lemons wedges,
   for squeezing

My take on a classic paella but with a lot less oil. If you don't fancy the mussels, you can leave them out and you'll save about 40 calories per serving.

Put the saffron in a measuring jug and add the just-boiled water and stock cube. Stir to dissolve the stock cube then leave to stand for about 10 minutes. Trim any visible fat off the chicken using kitchen scissors or a sharp knife. Cut each thigh in half.

Heat the oil in a large wide-based non-stick sauté pan, shallow flameproof casserole or paella pan over a medium heat. Fry the onion and peppers for 10 minutes until well softened and lightly browned, stirring regularly.

Add the chicken and chorizo, season well with salt and pepper and cook for 3 minutes more, stirring. Add the rice and paprika and cook for a few seconds. Pour over the saffron chicken stock and bring to a simmer. Cook for 15 minutes, stirring regularly until the rice is almost tender and the liquid is nearly absorbed.

While the rice is cooking, scrub the mussels really well and scrape off any barnacles. Remove the beards. Discard mussels that are damaged in any way or that are open and don't close when tapped on the side of the sink. Put the good mussels in a bowl.

Stir the mussels, prawns and parsley into the rice. Cover the pan with a lid or a large piece of foil and cook for a further 5–10 minutes, without stirring, or until the prawns are hot throughout, the mussels have opened and the rice is tender. Discard any mussels that haven't opened. Scatter chopped parsley over the top and serve with lemon wedges for squeezing.

490 CALORIES PER SERVING

linguine with scallops and prawns

SERVES 2
PREP: 10 MINUTES
COOK: 12 MINUTES

150g dried linguine
2 tbsp extra virgin olive oil
150g frozen roeless
    scallops, thawed
3 large garlic cloves,
    very thinly sliced
1 long red chilli, deseeded
    first if you like, thinly
    sliced, or 1 tsp dried
    chilli flakes
50ml white wine
100g raw, peeled king
    prawns, thawed if frozen
15g bunch of fresh flat-leaf
    parsley, leaves finely
    chopped
1 tbsp fresh lemon juice
flaked sea salt
ground black pepper
lemon wedges, for
    squeezing

This seafood pasta is a real treat when you are losing weight – it's a bit pricey but makes a very special meal for two. Tongs or a large spoon and fork work well for tossing and serving.

Half fill a large saucepan with cold water and bring it to the boil. Slowly add the linguine, pushing down and separating the strands as they enter the water. Stir well as the pasta begins to soften and return to the boil. Cook for 10–12 minutes, or according to the packet instructions, until just tender.

While the linguine is boiling, place a medium non-stick frying pan over a high heat and brush with 1 teaspoon of oil. Season the scallops on one side with the salt and pepper then place in the frying pan, seasoned side down. Season on the other side and cook for 1 minute.

Turn the scallops over and cook on the reverse side for 1 minute or until nicely browned but not quite cooked through. Transfer the scallops to a plate and return the pan to a low heat.

Add the remaining oil and very gently fry the garlic and chilli for 3 minutes or until well softened, stirring regularly. Pour the wine into the pan and bring it to a simmer. Add the prawns and simmer for 1–2 minutes, turning until they are cooked and pink throughout. Return the scallops to the pan and cook for 30 seconds more or until hot throughout. Take the pan off the heat.

Drain the pasta in a large colander and return it to the saucepan. Scatter over the chopped parsley, pour over the lemon juice, season with ground black pepper and toss. Tip the seafood mixture into the saucepan and toss everything well together. Serve in deep bowls with lemon wedges for squeezing.

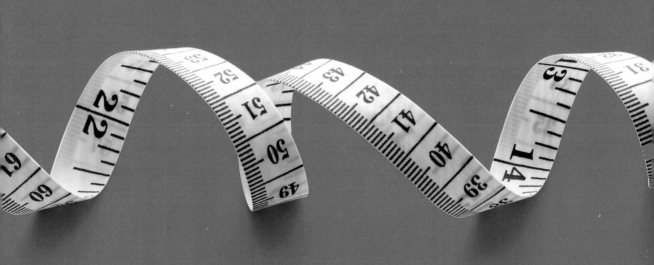

salads

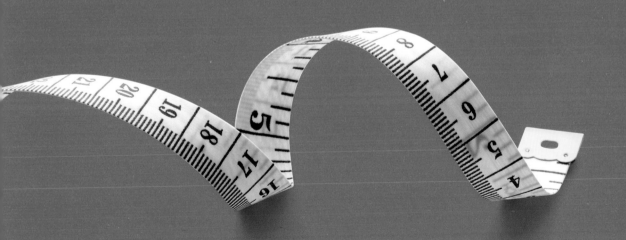

330
CALORIES
PER SERVING

sesame chicken
noodle salad

SERVES 4

**PREP: 15 MINUTES,
PLUS STANDING TIME**

COOK: 20 MINUTES

3 boneless, skinless chicken
    breasts (each about 150g)
½ tsp ground ginger
2 tbsp dark soy sauce
100g medium dried egg
    noodles
2 large carrots, peeled
100g mangetout, trimmed
    and halved lengthways
100g frozen soya beans
    or peas
6 spring onions, thinly sliced
½ tsp sesame seeds

FOR THE DRESSING
2 tbsp caster sugar
6 tbsp cold water
1–2 tsp red chilli paste
    (from a jar)
1 tbsp dark soy sauce
2 tsp toasted sesame oil

Tip: Red chilli paste is a
useful ingredient to keep
in the fridge and can be
stirred into all sorts of
dressings and sauces.
It saves the bother of
chopping fresh chillies
and you can also adjust the
amount of heat as you like.

Cold noodle salads make great packed lunches; this one can
be made a day ahead and will still taste fabulous. Look out
for packets of frozen soya beans (without their pods) as they
make an interesting and nutritious change from peas.

To make the dressing, put the sugar in a small saucepan with
the water and heat gently until dissolved. Bring to the boil
and cook for 1 minute, stirring. Take off the heat and stir in
the chilli paste, soy sauce and sesame oil. Tip the dressing
into a heatproof bowl and leave to cool.

Preheat the oven to 210°C/Fan 190°C/Gas 6½. Put the chicken
breasts in a small ovenproof dish or tin lined with foil and rub
them with the ginger. Brush with the soy sauce and season with
black pepper. Bake for 18–20 minutes or until cooked through
and lightly browned. Put the chicken on a board and allow to
rest for 10 minutes.

While the chicken is cooking, half fill a saucepan with water
and bring it to the boil. Add the noodles and cook for 3 minutes,
or according to the packet instructions, until tender, stirring
occasionally to separate the noodle strands. Drain in a colander
and rinse under running water until cold. Tip the noodles into
a large mixing bowl.

Cut the carrots into long, wide strips. Place the strips in a pile
on top of each other and cut them into long thin matchsticks.
(You could coarsely grate the carrots if you prefer.) Add the
carrots, mangetout and soya beans or peas to the salad
(there is no need to cook them first).

Slice the chicken widthways and add it to the noodles and
vegetables. Pour over the dressing and toss well together.
Add the spring onions and sesame seeds and toss lightly.
Stand for 10 minutes before serving or cover and chill.
Eat within 2 days.

418
CALORIES
PER SERVING

spiced chicken and rice salad

SERVES 3
PREP: 15 MINUTES,
PLUS CHILLING TIME
COOK: 25 MINUTES

600ml water
1 chicken stock cube
350g pack chicken breast
   mini fillets
1 tbsp olive oil, plus 1 tsp
1 medium onion, finely
   chopped
1 red pepper, deseeded
   and cut into roughly
   2cm chunks
1 orange or yellow pepper,
   deseeded and cut into
   roughly 2cm chunks
3 tsp medium curry powder
100g easy-cook long
   grain rice
25g sultanas
25g toasted flaked almonds
25g bunch fresh coriander,
   leaves roughly chopped
4 tbsp fresh lime juice
   (from 2 large limes)
flaked sea salt
ground black pepper

This is a great salad for a summer lunch and a brilliant dish for a packed lunch. Keep cool until you are ready to eat. You can use chicken breasts instead of mini fillets if you like. Poach whole for 15-20 minutes then slice into bite-sized pieces once cooled.

Heat the water in a large non-stick frying pan. Add the stock cube and stir until dissolved. When the water is at a gentle simmer, add the chicken mini fillets and poach in the water for 10 minutes. Drain in a sieve, retaining the poaching liquid. Put the chicken on a plate and leave to cool for 15 minutes, cover and chill in the fridge until cold (this will take around 30 minutes). Wipe the pan clean.

While the chicken is cooling, heat the teaspoon of oil in the same frying pan and gently fry the onion and peppers for 4–5 minutes, stirring occasionally until just softened. Add the sultanas and cook for 1 minute more, stirring. Remove from the heat and spread onto a plate. Cool for 15 minutes, then cover and place in the fridge until cold.

When the chicken and vegetables are cold, pour the reserved stock into a medium saucepan and bring to the boil. Stir in the rice and 2 teaspoons of the curry powder. Return to the boil and cook for about 10 minutes or until tender, stirring occasionally. Drain well in a sieve and rinse under running water until cold.

Transfer the rice to a large bowl. Cut the cooled chicken into bite-sized pieces and add to the rice. Stir in the cooled vegetables, sultanas, flaked almonds and coriander.

Make the dressing by whisking the lime juice, remaining curry powder and rest of the oil together. Season with a little salt and pepper. Pour over the salad and toss well together. Keep chilled until ready to serve.

399
CALORIES
PER SERVING

barbecue-style chicken pasta salad

SERVES 4
PREP: 15 MINUTES
COOK: 30 MINUTES

6 boneless, skinless chicken
   thighs (about 500g)
150g dried pasta shapes,
   such as penne or fusilli
198g can sweetcorn,
   drained
2 little gem lettuces, leaves
   separated and halved
150g cherry tomatoes,
   halved
1/3 cucumber, cut into
   small chunks
flaked sea salt
ground black pepper

FOR THE BARBECUE SAUCE
3 tbsp tomato ketchup
1½ tbsp clear honey
1 tbsp Worcestershire sauce
1 tsp smoked paprika
¼ tsp hot chilli powder

FOR THE DRESSING
1 tbsp cold water
3 tbsp reduced-fat (light)
   mayonnaise

Sweet, sticky chicken, pasta and a simple salad make a magic combination that appeals to all ages. Brilliant if you are looking for a new lunchbox idea too.

Preheat the oven to 200°C/Fan 180°C/Gas 6. Line the base and sides of a baking tray with a piece of foil (this will stop the sauce sticking and making the tray difficult to clean).

Put the chicken thighs on a board and snip off any visible fat with a pair of kitchen scissors. Place the thighs on the lined tray, arranging them into nice neat shapes. Season with salt and pepper and bake for 15 minutes.

To make the barbecue sauce, mix the ketchup, honey, Worcestershire sauce, paprika and chilli powder together. Take the baking tray out of the oven and brush the sauce liberally over the chicken. Return the tray to the oven and bake for a further 15 minutes or until the chicken is cooked throughout and the sauce is sticky and glossy.

While the chicken is cooking, half fill a medium pan with water and bring it to the boil. Add the pasta, stir and return to the boil. Cook for 10–12 minutes, or according to the packet instructions, until tender, stirring occasionally.

Drain the pasta in a sieve and rinse under running water until cold. Put the pasta in a large bowl and toss with the sweetcorn, lettuce, tomatoes and cucumber. For the dressing, mix the water and mayonnaise together in a small bowl until smooth.

Transfer the cooked chicken to a board and slice thickly. Scatter the slices over the salad, drizzle with the dressing and serve immediately. If you want to serve the salad cold, leave the chicken to cool completely on the board before adding it to the salad. Drizzle with the dressing just before serving.

431
CALORIES
PER SERVING

pesto chicken pasta salad

SERVES 4

PREP: 15 MINUTES

COOK: 10–15 MINUTES

200g dried pasta shapes,
   such as penne, fusilli
   or cavatappi
2 cooked, skinless, boneless
   chicken breasts (each
   about 100g)
2 tbsp sun-dried tomato
   pesto (from a jar)
50g mayonnaise
150g fat-free Greek yoghurt
1 tbsp cold water
100g mixed spinach,
   watercress and
   rocket salad
25g pine nuts
ground black pepper

Tips: The pine nuts taste
even more delicious if they
are toasted. Simply place
them in a small frying pan
and cook them over a
medium heat, turning them
frequently for 4–5 minutes
or until lightly browned.
Cool before sprinkling
over the salad.

You can buy ready-cooked
chicken breasts in the
supermarket or prepare
your own chicken. This
recipe is also a great way
to use up leftover chicken.

This is one of those recipes in which the full-fat mayonnaise
seems to work a little better than the light one. The fat-free
Greek yoghurt will help reduce the overall calories for the
dressing and adds a nice tanginess to the salad.

Half fill a large saucepan with water and bring it to the boil.
Tip the pasta into the boiling water and cook for 10–12 minutes,
or according to the packet instructions, until tender, stirring
occasionally.

Meanwhile, slice the cooked chicken and put it in a bowl.
Toss with 1 tablespoon of the pesto sauce. Make the dressing
by mixing the mayonnaise, yoghurt, the remaining tablespoon
of pesto sauce and water in a small bowl.

Drain the pasta in a colander and rinse under running water
until cold. Tip into a large bowl and toss with the salad leaves
and sliced chicken. Spoon over the dressing and sprinkle with
pine nuts just before serving.

SALAD **133**

205 CALORIES PER SERVING

prawn and pasta layer salad

SERVES 4
PREP: 10 MINUTES
COOK: 8 MINUTES

50g small pasta shapes, such as little shells or rigati
4 tbsp reduced fat (light) mayonnaise
3 tbsp fat-free fromage frais
2 tbsp tomato ketchup
200g cooked and peeled cold water prawns, thawed and drained if frozen
1 medium carrot (about 100g), peeled and coarsely grated
198g can sweetcorn, drained
¼ cucumber, cut into roughly 1.5cm chunks
¼ iceberg lettuce, shredded
flaked sea salt
ground black pepper

Perfect for lunchboxes and picnics, this popular prawn salad can be made the evening before if you like and tossed lightly just before serving.

Half fill a medium saucepan with water and bring it to the boil. Add the pasta, stir well and return to the boil. Cook for 8 minutes, or according to the packet instructions, until tender, stirring occasionally.

Mix the mayonnaise, fromage frais and ketchup together in a medium bowl. Stir in the prawns and season with salt and pepper. Rinse the pasta in a colander under running water until cold and drain well. Divide the pasta between 4 lidded containers or serve in a large glass bowl. Top the pasta with first the carrot, then the sweetcorn, then the cucumber.

Place the shredded lettuce on top and divide the prawns and sauce between the containers or bowl. Cover tightly and keep chilled until ready to serve. Toss lightly to serve.

332
CALORIES
PER SERVING

lime and coriander
salmon salad

SERVES 2

PREP: 10 MINUTES

COOK: 10 MINUTES

50g basmati rice
100g long-stemmed
  broccoli, trimmed and
  each stem cut into three
2 small little gem lettuces,
  separated into leaves
15g bunch of fresh
  coriander, leaves chopped
150g kiln-roasted or
  poached salmon

FOR THE DRESSING
1½ tbsp fresh lime juice
  (from 1 large lime)
1 tsp caster sugar
1 tbsp dark soy sauce
pinch of flaked sea salt
1 tbsp sunflower oil
ground black pepper

Tip: Choose roasted salmon
from the chiller cabinet –
the kind that is lightly
smoked too if you can find
it. Otherwise, bake a couple
of salmon fillets on a baking
tray in a moderate oven for
about 15 minutes and leave
them to cool before flaking
on top of the salad.

A light zingy salad that makes a wonderful, fresh-tasting packed lunch or summer salad. It's one of our favourites in the test kitchen because it's so easy and quick to prepare.

Half fill a medium saucepan with water and bring it to the boil. Put the rice in a sieve and rinse under plenty of cold water – this will get rid of excess starch and help to keep the grains separate as they cook.

Add the rice to the water, stir well and return to the boil. Cook for 8 minutes. Add the broccoli and cook with the rice for 2 minutes more or until the rice is tender, stirring occasionally.

While the rice is cooking, make the dressing. Pour the lime juice into a small bowl and whisk in the sugar, soy sauce, a pinch of salt and some ground black pepper. Slowly whisk in the oil until the dressing is slightly thickened.

Divide the lettuce leaves between 2 bowls or lidded containers. Rinse the rice and broccoli in a sieve under running water until cold. Drain thoroughly and toss lightly with the coriander. Spoon on top of the lettuce leaves. Add the salmon, flaked into chunky pieces, and spoon over the dressing just before serving.

223

CALORIES
PER SERVING

prawn noodle salad

SERVES 2
PREP: 20 MINUTES
COOK: 3–5 MINUTES

40g fine dried rice noodles
(vermicelli noodle nests)
150g cooked and peeled
cold water prawns,
thawed if frozen and
drained
¼ cucumber, cut into
roughly 1.5cm chunks
2 medium carrots, peeled
and coarsely grated
2 spring onions, trimmed
and thinly sliced
1 long red chilli, thinly sliced
(deseed first if you like)
20g bunch of fresh
coriander
20g bunch of fresh mint

FOR THE DRESSING
1 tbsp Thai fish sauce
(nam pla)
1 tbsp soft light brown
sugar
1 tbsp fresh lime juice
½ tsp dried chilli flakes

Tips: If you don't like your
food too spicy, leave out the
chilli or deseed it before
slicing. Make sure you wash
your hands really well after
preparing the chilli.

Coarsely grate the carrot in
an upright position so the
strips will be longer and
more elegant.

**Full of fresh, lively flavours and plenty of heat. This salad
makes a great packed lunch but remember to toss the herbs
through just before serving as they could become soggy
otherwise.**

Put the rice noodles in a heatproof bowl and pour over just-
boiled water from a kettle to cover. Leave to stand for
3–5 minutes, or according to the packet instructions, then drain
in a sieve and rinse under running water until cold.

While the noodles are softening, put the dressing ingredients
into a bowl and whisk them together. Add the prawns,
cucumber, carrots, spring onions and red chilli.

Strip the leaves off the herbs, tearing any large leaves in half,
and scatter them on top of the prawn mixture. Add the noodles
and toss everything together lightly. Divide between 2 dishes
and serve immediately.

333 CALORIES PER SERVING

tomato, basil and mozzarella pasta salad

SERVES 4
PREP: 10 MINUTES
COOK: 10 MINUTES

200g dried pasta shapes, such as gigli or penne
4 large ripe tomatoes, each cut into 8 wedges
125g ball mozzarella, drained
1 small growing basil plant or 20g bunch of fresh basil
3 tbsp fresh basil pesto sauce (from the chiller cabinet)
1 tbsp cold water
ground black pepper

A colourful pasta salad with a quick basil dressing, this makes a great lunch or light supper dish. Take your tomatoes out of the fridge a few hours before making the salad and they'll have lots more flavour.

Half fill a large saucepan with water and bring it to the boil. Add the pasta, stir well and return to the boil. Cook for 10–12 minutes, or according to the packet instructions, until tender, stirring occasionally.

Drain the pasta in a colander under running water until cold, then tip into a large serving bowl or platter. Add the tomatoes and tear the mozzarella into bite-sized pieces on top. Season with freshly ground black pepper.

Strip the leaves off the basil plant or tear the fresh basil leaves and scatter over the pasta. Toss lightly together. Mix the pesto with the water in a small bowl and spoon over the top. Serve immediately.

159
CALORIES
PER SERVING

mediterranean vegetable and giant couscous salad

SERVES 4

PREP: 10 MINUTES

COOKING: 12 MINUTES

oil, for brushing or spraying
2 small courgettes, trimmed
   and cut into roughly
   1.5cm slices
1 large red pepper,
   deseeded and cut into
   roughly 2cm chunks
1 large yellow pepper,
   deseeded and cut into
   roughly 2cm chunks
1 medium red onion, peeled
   and cut into 12 wedges
100g dried giant couscous
25g rocket leaves
flaked sea salt
ground black pepper

FOR THE DRESSING
1 tbsp chipotle paste
   (from a jar)
2 tbsp fresh lemon juice
1 tbsp extra virgin olive oil

Chipotle paste makes a fantastic base for the dressing for this simple salad. Its smoky heat really complements the zingy lemon and lightly charred vegetables. You'll find it in the Mexican section of the supermarket and online. You can also serve this salad as a starter to serve 6, which will take the calorie count down to 106 per serving.

Heat a large non-stick frying pan or wok over a high heat and brush or spray lightly with oil. Add the vegetables to the pan, spray with a little more oil and stir-fry for about 6–8 minutes or until they have softened, are nicely coloured and a little charred in places. Season with salt and pepper, tip into a large serving bowl and leave to cool.

Half fill a medium saucepan with water and bring it to the boil. Add the giant couscous, stir and return to the boil. Cook for 5 minutes or until tender. Drain in a sieve under running water until cold. Add the couscous to the vegetables. Toss lightly and scatter the rocket leaves over the top. Cover and chill until ready to serve.

In a small bowl, mix the chipotle paste with the lemon juice and the olive oil. Pour over the salad and toss lightly just before serving.

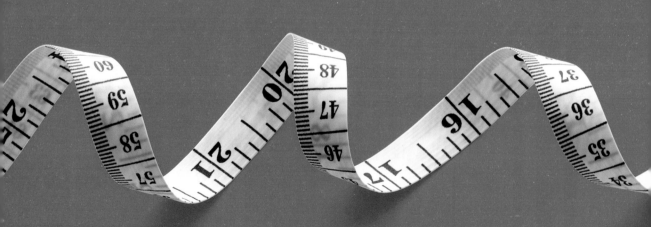

sauces
for pasta

133
CALORIES
PER SERVING

fresh tomato sauce

SERVES 2

PREP: 10 MINUTES

COOK: 7 MINUTES

300g mixed tomatoes,
  different sizes and colours
  if possible
2 tbsp extra virgin olive oil
1 garlic clove, peeled and
  very thinly sliced
2 tbsp cold water (optional)
10g bunch of fresh oregano
2 bushy sprigs of fresh
  young thyme
½ tsp caster sugar
¼–½ tsp flaked sea salt
ground black pepper

A light and fresh-tasting sauce that makes the most of seasonal tomatoes when they are cheapest. Perfect if you grow a few of your own. Don't overcook the tomatoes; they should be softened and juicy but not completely falling apart. Cook 50g of dried pasta for each person, but don't forget to add the extra calories.

Cut cherry tomatoes in half and quarter or cut larger tomatoes into wedges.

Heat the oil in a medium non-stick frying pan over a very low heat. Add the garlic, tomatoes and water and cook gently for 5 minutes, stirring regularly until the tomatoes are softened but still holding their shape.

While the tomatoes are cooking, strip the oregano and thyme leaves off their stalks. Stir the herbs, sugar, salt and black pepper to taste into the tomatoes and cook for 1 minute more. Toss through freshly cooked pasta.

126
CALORIES
PER SERVING

magic cauliflower sauce

SERVES 4

PREP: 15 MINUTES

COOK: 15 MINUTES

275g small cauliflower
  florets
25g butter, plus extra
  for greasing
25g plain flour
300ml semi-skimmed milk
flaked sea salt
ground black pepper

Flat freeze the cooked
and cooled sauce in freezer
bags for up to 3 months.
Rinse the bags under hot
water for a few seconds
then break the frozen sauce
into a wide-based, non-stick
saucepan, add a splash of
water and reheat, stirring
regularly until piping hot
throughout.

Tip: A 700g cauliflower with
leaves should give you
about 275g of florets. If you
don't have a stick blender,
blitz the cauliflower really
well in a food processor
after cooling for a few
minutes or pass it through
a sieve.

This is my magic cauliflower sauce that makes any pasta dish
taste extra creamy and delicious. Swap for a high-fat cheesy
sauce in your usual lasagne or macaroni cheese, or toss
through freshly cooked pasta and a few vegetables. It also
freezes well, so have some handy to reheat from frozen. One
batch makes about 350ml of sauce – the same as those little
tubs you can buy in the supermarket.

Half fill a large saucepan with water and bring it to the boil.
Add the cauliflower, return to the boil and cook for 10–12
minutes or until very soft.

Meanwhile, melt the butter in a medium non-stick saucepan
over a low heat then stir in the flour and cook for 30 seconds,
stirring continuously.

Gradually stir in the milk and bring to a gentle simmer. Cook for
3-5 minutes or until the sauce is thickened and smooth, stirring
continuously. Season with a little salt and some ground black
pepper. Remove from the heat.

Add the cooked cauliflower to the pan with the sauce. Using
a stick blender, blitz the cauliflower into the sauce until it is as
smooth as possible. Return to the heat. Warm through gently,
adding a little more seasoning or a dash of milk if necessary. It
should have the consistency of pouring custard.

96
CALORIES
PER SERVING

simple tomato pasta sauce

**SERVES 4
(MAKES 600ML)
PREP: 10 MINUTES
COOK: 40 MINUTES**

1 tbsp olive oil
2 medium onions, finely
    chopped
3 garlic cloves, crushed
2 x 400g cans chopped
    tomatoes
2 tsp dried oregano
¼ tsp dried chilli flakes
1 tbsp clear honey or
    2 tsp soft brown sugar
1 large bay leaf
½ tsp fine sea salt
ground black pepper

Flat freeze the cooked
and cooled sauce in freezer
bags for up to 3 months.
Rinse the bags under hot
water for a few seconds
then break the frozen sauce
into a wide-based, non-stick
saucepan, add a splash of
water and reheat, stirring
regularly until piping hot
throughout.

A great basic tomato sauce that can be used as a base for
all kinds of pasta dishes. Flat freeze some sauce so you can
reheat it from frozen and you'll never be stuck for something
quick for supper – it could save you a fortune in takeaway
meals and trips to the local supermarket.

Heat the oil in a large non-stick saucepan. Add the onions,
cover loosely with a lid and cook over a low heat for 10 minutes
until well softened and lightly browned, stirring occasionally.
Stir in the garlic and cook for 1 minute more.

Add the tomatoes, oregano, chilli flakes, honey or sugar and the
bay leaf. Stir well and season with the salt and plenty of freshly
ground pepper.

Bring to a gentle simmer and cook, uncovered, for 30 minutes
or until the sauce is rich and thick, stirring occasionally. Discard
the bay leaf and tweak the seasoning to taste.

130
CALORIES
PER SERVING

creamy tomato and chilli pasta sauce

SERVES 4
(MAKES 600ML)
PREP: 10 MINUTES
COOK: 40 MINUTES

1 tbsp olive oil
1 medium onion, finely
    chopped
2 garlic cloves, crushed
1 long red chilli, finely
    chopped (deseed first if
    you like)
2 x 400g cans chopped
    tomatoes
2 tsp dried oregano
25g fresh basil leaves,
    finely shredded (optional)
½ tsp fine sea salt
3 tbsp double cream
ground black pepper

Flat freeze the cooked
and cooled sauce in freezer
bags for up to 4 months.
Rinse the bags under hot
water for a few seconds
then break the frozen sauce
into a wide-based, non-stick
saucepan, add a splash of
water and reheat, stirring
regularly, until piping hot
throughout.

Tip: If your fresh chilli isn't
particularly hot – taste a
tiny section from the end
to give you an indication –
you may need to add
½–1 teaspoon of dried chilli
flakes or ½ teaspoon of hot
chilli powder when you add
the garlic.

I love a creamy tomato and chilli pasta sauce but it can be
loaded with calories, so try making this fiery sauce instead.
I've kept the cream quantity as low as possible, adding just
enough to temper the heat from the chilli. If the sauce is still
a little too hot for your taste, add some extra cream once
it is tossed with the pasta, but don't forget to increase the
calories per serving by about 75 for every tablespoon you use.

Heat the oil in a large non-stick saucepan. Add the onion, cover
loosely with a lid and cook over a low heat for 10 minutes until
well softened and lightly browned, stirring occasionally. Stir in
the garlic and chilli and cook for a few seconds more.

Add the tomatoes, oregano and basil, if using. Season with
the salt and plenty of freshly ground pepper. Bring to a gentle
simmer and cook, uncovered, for 30 minutes or until the sauce
is rich and thick, stirring occasionally. Stir in the cream and
cook for a few seconds more, stirring. Adjust the seasoning
before adding to pasta.

102

mushroom sauce for pasta

SERVES 4

**PREP: 5 MINUTES,
PLUS SOAKING TIME**

COOK: 10 MINUTES

5g dried porcini mushrooms
200ml just-boiled water
2 tsp sunflower oil
250g Portobello or field
    mushrooms (4 large),
    peeled, cut in half and
    sliced
15g butter
25g plain flour
2 tbsp Madeira or Marsala
    wine
150ml semi-skimmed milk
flaked sea salt
ground black pepper
chopped flat leaf parsley,
    to garnish

A full-flavoured mushroom sauce that's made with a combination of dried and fresh Portobello mushrooms. Madeira really complements the other flavours but you could add a dash of sherry or white wine if you prefer – or leave it out altogether.

Put the dried mushrooms in a measuring jug and cover with the just-boiled water. Leave to stand for 20 minutes. Drain in a sieve and reserve the liquor. Put the mushrooms on a board and roughly chop them.

Heat the oil in a medium non-stick frying pan and fry the Portobello mushrooms over a high heat for 3–5 minutes until lightly browned. Season well with salt and pepper.

Reduce the heat, stir in the butter and, as soon as it has melted, add the flour and the soaked, chopped mushrooms and cook for a few seconds, stirring.

Add the mushroom liquor, just a little at a time, stirring well in between each addition and taking care to avoid adding any gritty bits from the bottom of the jug.

Slowly add the Madeira or Marsala and the milk, a little at a time, stirring continuously. Then bring the sauce to a simmer and cook for 2 minutes, stirring. Adjust the seasoning to taste and toss through freshly cooked pasta (don't forget to add the extra calories). Garnish with chopped parsley if you like.

91
CALORIES
PER SERVING

broccoli pesto

SERVES 6

PREP: 10 MINUTES

COOK: 5 MINUTES

150g broccoli florets
50g basil leaves
1 large garlic clove, peeled
   and crushed
25g Parmesan cheese,
   finely grated
25g pine nuts
2 tbsp extra virgin olive oil
flaked sea salt
ground black pepper

Flat freeze the cooked
and cooled sauce in freezer
bags for up to 3 months.
Rinse the bags under hot
water for a few seconds
then break the frozen sauce
into a wide-based, non-stick
saucepan, add a splash of
water and reheat, stirring
regularly until hot.

**My broccoli pesto is lower in fat and calories than the usual kind
and because it's made with a broccoli base, you are getting
extra vitamins and fibre too. Freeze what you don't use.**

Half fill a medium saucepan with water and bring it to the boil.
Add the broccoli and return to the boil. Cook for 5 minutes
or until it is only just tender. Rinse in a colander under running
water until cold then drain well.

Put the broccoli in a food processor with the basil, garlic
and Parmesan. Season with salt and ground black pepper
and blend until almost smooth.

Add the pine nuts and the oil and blend on the pulse setting
until combined. Adjust the seasoning to taste, then spoon into
a bowl. This pesto will keep for a couple of days in the fridge
and can be tossed through pasta, mixed with mashed potato
and tossed with new potatoes too.

53
CALORIES
PER SERVING

sweet roasted tomatoes and thyme

SERVES 4

PREP: 5 MINUTES

COOK: 1 HOUR 10 MINUTES

oil, for brushing or spraying
500g small, ripe tomatoes
    (not cherry tomatoes)
1 heaped tbsp fresh young
    thyme leaves
1 tbsp extra virgin olive oil
20g fresh basil leaves,
    roughly torn
flaked sea salt
freshly ground black pepper

Tomatoes are naturally low in calories and when roasted they make a wonderful sauce for pasta – all you need to add is a little olive oil, a handful of fresh basil and ground black pepper. The cooked tomatoes will keep for about three days in the fridge, so you can use them for salads and plates of antipasti too.

Preheat the oven to 200°C/Fan 180°C/Gas 6. Brush or spray a baking tray with oil. Cut the tomatoes in half and place them cut side up on the tray. Season generously with salt and pepper.

Bake for 30 minutes then reduce the heat to 160°C/Fan 140°C/Gas 3 and cook for a further 30–40 minutes or until the tomatoes are semi-dried and lightly browned in places. Sprinkle with the thyme.

Toss the warm tomatoes, basil and olive oil through freshly cooked pasta and serve with a large mixed salad. Alternatively, leave to cool and use for pasta salads.

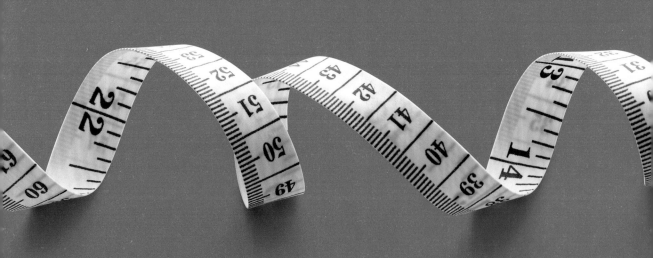

sweet
things

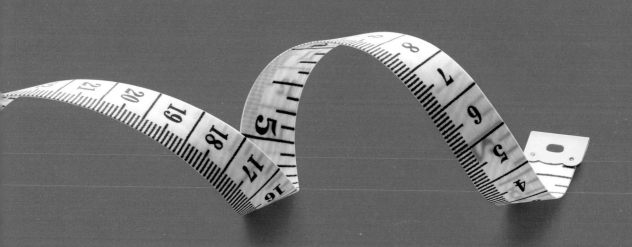

146
CALORIES
PER SERVING

lemon rice puddings with raspberries

SERVES 6

PREP: 5 MINUTES

COOK: 20 MINUTES

125g pudding rice
600ml semi-skimmed milk
1 tsp vanilla extract
300ml cold water
3 tbsp lemon curd
150g fresh or frozen
    raspberries, thawed
    if frozen

A cooling dessert of cold, creamy-tasting rice, flavoured with tangy lemon curd and topped with raspberries.

Put the rice, 400ml of the milk, the vanilla and the water in a medium non-stick saucepan and bring to a gentle simmer over a low heat. Cook for about 20 minutes, stirring regularly, until the rice is tender and the sauce is creamy.

Stir frequently towards the end of the cooking time as the mixture will thicken. (It will also continue to thicken as it cools.) Take the pan off the heat and stir in the remaining 200ml of cold milk and the lemon curd. Pour into 6 small dishes and leave to cool. Cover and place in the fridge for at least 2 hours or until well chilled.

Uncover the puddings and top with the raspberries just before serving. Covered and kept in the fridge, these puddings should keep well for up to 3 days.

209
CALORIES
PER SERVING

spiced apple rice pudding

SERVES 5
PREP: 10 MINUTES
COOK: 20 MINUTES

125g pudding rice
600ml semi-skimmed milk
200ml cold water
2 tsp vanilla extract
  or vanilla bean paste

FOR THE TOPPING
2 Bramley cooking apples
  (each about 250g)
1 tbsp fresh lemon juice
1 tbsp cold water
¼ tsp ground cinnamon,
  plus extra for sprinkling
2 tbsp caster sugar
40g sultanas

Pots of chilled rice pudding are quite expensive to buy and yet simple to make. The vanilla will help the rice taste sweet, so there should be no need for additional sugar.

Put the rice, milk, water and vanilla in a medium non-stick saucepan and bring to a gentle simmer over a medium heat. Cook for 16–18 minutes, or until the rice is tender and the sauce is creamy, stirring regularly.

Stir frequently towards the end of the cooking time as the mixture will thicken. (It will also continue to thicken as it cools.) Serve warm or cover the surface of the rice with cling film and leave to cool.

To make the topping, peel, quarter and core the apples, then roughly chop them into 1.5cm chunks. Put the apple in a saucepan with the lemon juice, water, cinnamon and sugar and bring to a gentle simmer. Cook for 5 minutes, stirring gently until the apples are very soft. Stir in the sultanas and cook for 1 minute more, stirring.

Spoon the rice pudding into tumblers or dessert dishes and top with the warm apple compote, sprinkle with cinnamon and serve immediately, or leave to cool then swirl with the apple.

154
CALORIES
PER FINGER

shortbread fingers

MAKES 16
PREP: 10 MINUTES
COOK: 25 MINUTES

150g well-softened butter
75g golden caster sugar
200g plain flour
100g ground rice

Freeze the cooked and cooled shortbread in a freezer-proof container for up to 3 months. Place as many as you need on a baking tray and warm through in a moderate oven for about 10 minutes. Cool for 10 minutes and serve.

Tip: This shortbread makes a lovely dessert when served with a bowl of fresh berries – blackcurrants are my favourite – and half-fat crème fraiche. You can sweeten the fruit with a fine dusting of icing sugar if you like.

Shortbread fingers are traditionally very high in fat and sugar. I've managed to reduce the fat and sugar in my recipe by about 25%, but they still taste so good, no one will guess. It's worth going easy on them nevertheless, as they remain fairly high in calories. Freeze any that aren't served immediately and keep them out of temptation's way!

Preheat the oven to 180°C/Fan 160°C/Gas 4. Line the base of a 20cm square, loose-based cake or brownie tin with baking parchment.

Put the butter and sugar in a large bowl and beat them with a wooden spoon or an electric whisk until smooth and pale. Add the plain flour and ground rice and beat until the ingredients come together and form a loose, crumbly mixture, a bit like damp sand.

Tip the mixture into the prepared tin and press the surface to make it as smooth as possible, using your hands or the back of a dessertspoon.

Prick the shortbread in neat lines with a fork. Bake for 25 minutes or until firm and pale golden brown. Mark into 16 fingers with a sharp knife then leave to cool completely.

Once cold, lift the shortbread out of the tin, keeping it on the base, and cut it into fingers. Keep the shortbread in an airtight container and eat within 5 days.

172
CALORIES
PER SERVING

roasted figs with rose rice

SERVES 6

**PREP: 10 MINUTES,
PLUS CHILLING TIME**

COOK: 15-17 MINUTES

65g ground rice
650ml semi-skimmed milk
2 tbsp clear honey
2 long strips of lemon rind
3 tbsp single cream
1 tsp rose water

FOR THE TOPPING
6 ripe figs
25g pistachio nuts,
   roughly chopped
2 tbsp clear honey

This dish is based on muhallabia, a Middle Eastern dessert made from ground rice and flavoured with rose water. It's usually made with full-fat milk, cream and almonds, but my lower calorie version still has a lovely creamy texture and is made extra delicious when topped with roasted figs and pistachio nuts.

Put the rice in a medium non-stick saucepan and stir in 6 tablespoons of the milk. Mix with a wooden spoon to make a smooth paste then slowly pour in 450ml of the remaining milk, stirring all the time. Add the honey and lemon rind and place the pan over a low heat.

Bring the milk to a gentle simmer and cook for 5 minutes or until well thickened and almost smooth, stirring continuously. (The ground rice should soften and swell as it cooks.) Take the pan off the heat and stir in the rest of the milk, the cream and the rose water.

Pour the rice custard into 6–8 heatproof glass dishes or tumblers and cool for 10 minutes. Cover and place in the fridge for at least 1 hour to chill.

Preheat the oven to 200°C/Fan 180°C/Gas 6. Cut the figs in half from stem to base and place them on a small foil-lined baking tray, cut side up. Sprinkle with the nuts and drizzle with honey. Bake for 10 minutes until softened and sticky. Serve the figs hot or cold with the chilled rice pudding.

179
CALORIES
PER SERVING

apple noodle kugel

SERVES 6

PREP: 15 MINUTES

COOK: 45 MINUTES

150g dried wide, flat pasta
strips (pappardelle)
2 Bramley cooking apples
(each about 250g)
2 eating apples (each
about 200g)
½ tsp ground cinnamon
50g sultanas
oil for spraying or brushing
15g butter
1 tbsp caster sugar (ideally
golden caster sugar)

Kugel noodles are a baked dish that usually combines cooked pasta with soft cheese, eggs, sugar and spices before baking. Mine is made using apples as well to keep the calories low. It's a bit like an apple strudel but much easier to prepare.

Preheat the oven to 200°C/Fan 180°C/Gas 6. Half fill a large saucepan with water and bring it to the boil. Add the pasta, stir and return to the boil. Cook for about 5–7 minutes, or according to the packet instructions, until tender, stirring occasionally.

While the pasta is cooking, peel, quarter and core the apples and then cut them into thin slices. Put the apple slices in a large bowl and toss them with the cinnamon and sultanas.

Drain the pasta in a colander and rinse under running water until cold. Drain well and mix with the apples and sultanas. Tip into a lightly oiled roasting tin or ovenproof dish roughly 20 x 30cm.

Cover the dish with foil and bake for 30 minutes or until the apples are well softened. Take the tin or dish out of the oven, remove the foil and dot with small pieces of butter. Sprinkle with the sugar, return to the oven and bake without covering for a further 10 minutes or until the apples are lightly browned. Serve with half-fat crème fraiche, single cream or lower fat vanilla ice cream, but don't forget to add the extra calories.

64
CALORIES
PER CAKE

florentine rice cakes

MAKES 9
PREP: 10 MINUTES,
PLUS COOLING TIME
COOK: 5 MINUTES

50g orange-flavoured
   dark chocolate, broken
   into pieces
9 unsalted, wholegrain
   thin rice cakes (each
   about 4.5g)
10g chopped shelled
   pistachio nuts
10g toasted flaked almonds
15g cut mixed peel

A great way to jazz up bought rice cakes and delicious served with coffee, this version is topped with drizzles of orange-flavoured chocolate and topped with a mixture of nuts and candied peel – the kind you find in the baking aisle of the supermarket. Choose the extra thin rice cakes as they are only about 18 calories each.

Melt the chocolate in a heatproof bowl set over a saucepan of gently simmering water or in the microwave. Place the rice cakes on a rack over a tray.

Use a teaspoon to drizzle the melted chocolate over the rice cakes. Sprinkle with the nuts and fruit. Leave the chocolate to set in a cool place, or the fridge, for 30 minutes or until solid. Store in an airtight tin, interleaved with baking parchment and eat within 2 days.

162
CALORIES
PER SERVING

chocolate risotto cups

SERVES 6

PREP: 5 MINUTES

COOK: 20-25 MINUTES

125g Arborio (risotto) rice
    or pudding rice
550ml semi-skimmed milk
100ml cold water
1½ tsp vanilla extract
50g plain dark chocolate
    (about 70% cocoa solids),
    coarsely grated

You can use either risotto rice or pudding rice for this simple chocolate pudding. The risotto rice tends to keeps its shape and stay a little firmer than the pudding rice, but there's not much in it, so use whichever you have handy. Serve topped with a few fresh berries if you like.

Put the rice, milk, water and vanilla in a medium non-stick saucepan and bring to a gentle simmer over a medium heat. Cook for 20–25 minutes, stirring regularly, until the rice is tender and the sauce is creamy.

Stir frequently towards the end of the cooking time as the mixture will thicken. (Don't forget that it will continue to thicken as it cools.)

Remove from the heat and lightly stir in two-thirds of the grated chocolate. Spoon the rice pudding into heatproof dishes or espresso coffee cups and serve warm, sprinkled with the remaining chocolate. If serving cold, leave to cool then sprinkle with the remaining grated chocolate to decorate.

a few notes on
the recipes

INGREDIENTS

Where possible, choose free-range chicken, meat and eggs. Eggs used in the recipes are medium unless otherwise stated.

All poultry and meat has been trimmed of as much hard or visible fat as possible, although there may be some marbling within the meat. Boneless, skinless chicken breasts weigh about 175g. Fish has been scaled, gutted and pin-boned, and large prawns are deveined. You'll be able to buy most fish and seafood ready prepared but ask your fishmonger if not and they will be happy to help.

PREPARATION

Do as much preparation as possible before you start to cook. Discard any damaged bits, and wipe or wash fresh produce before preparation unless it's going to be peeled.

Onions, garlic and shallots are peeled unless otherwise stated, and vegetables are trimmed. Lemons, limes and oranges should be well washed before the zest is grated. Weigh fresh herbs in a bunch, then trim off the stalks before chopping the leaves. I've used medium-sized vegetables unless stated. As a rule of thumb, a medium-sized onion and potato (such as Maris Piper) weighs about 150g.

All chopped and sliced meat, poultry, fish and vegetable sizes are approximate. Don't worry if your pieces are a bit larger or smaller than indicated, but try to keep to roughly the size so the cooking times are accurate. Even-sized pieces will cook at the same rate, which is especially important for meat and fish.

I love using fresh herbs in my recipes, but you can substitute frozen herbs in most cases. Dried herbs will give a different, more intense flavour, so use them sparingly.

The recipes have been tested using sunflower oil, but you can substitute vegetable, groundnut or mild olive oil. I use dark soy sauce in the test kitchen but it's fine to use light instead – it'll give a milder flavour.

CALORIE COUNTS

Nutritional information does not include the optional serving suggestions. When shopping, you may see calories described as kilocalories on food labels; they are the same thing.

HOW TO FREEZE

Freezing food will save you time and money, and lots of the dishes in this book freeze extremely well. If you don't need all the servings at the same time, freeze the rest for another day. Where there are no instructions for freezing a dish, freezing won't give the best results once reheated.

When freezing food, it's important to cool it rapidly after cooking. Separate what you want to freeze from what you're going to serve and place it in a shallow, freezer-proof container. The shallower the container, the quicker the food will cool (putting it in the freezer while it's still warm will raise the freezer temperature and could affect other foods). Cover loosely, then freeze as soon as it's cool.

If you're freezing a lot of food at once, for example after a bulk cooking session or a big shop, flip the fast freeze button on at least two hours before adding the new dishes and leave it on for twenty-four hours afterwards. This will reduce the temperature of your freezer and help ensure that food is frozen as rapidly as possible.

When freezing food, expel as much air as possible by wrapping it tightly in a freezer bag or foil to help prevent icy patches, freezer burn and discolouration, or flavour transfer between dishes. Liquids expand when frozen, so leave a 4–5cm gap at the top of containers.

If you have a small freezer and need to save space, flat-freeze thick soups, sauces and casseroles in strong zip-seal freezer bags. Fill the bag a third full, then turn it over and flatten it until it is around 1–2cm thick, pressing out as much air as possible and sealing firmly.

Place delicate foods such as breaded chicken or fish fillets and burgers on a tray lined with baking parchment, and freeze in a single layer until solid before placing in containers or freezer bags. This method is called open freezing and helps stop foods sticking together in a block, so you can grab what you need easily.

Label everything clearly, and add the date so you know when to eat it at its best. I aim to use food from the freezer within about four months.

DEFROSTING

For the best results, most foods should be defrosted slowly in the fridge for several hours or overnight. For safety's sake, do not thaw dishes at room temperature.

Flat-frozen foods (see page 177) will thaw and begin to reheat at almost the same time. Just rinse the bag under hot water and break the mixture into a wide-based pan. Add a dash of water and warm over a low heat until thawed. Increase the heat, adding a little more water if necessary, and simmer until piping hot throughout, stirring occasionally.

Ensure that any perishable foods that have been frozen are thoroughly cooked or reheated before serving.

HOW TO GET THE BEST RESULTS
Measuring with spoons

Spoon measurements are level unless otherwise stated. Use a set of measuring spoons for the best results; they're endlessly useful, especially if you're watching your sugar, salt or fat intake.

1 tsp (1 teaspoon) = 5ml
1 dsp (1 dessertspoon) = 10ml
1 tbsp (1 tablespoon) = 15ml

A scant measure is just below level and a heaped measure is just above. An Australian tablespoon holds 20ml, so Australian cooks should use three level teaspoon measures instead.

CONVERSION CHARTS
Oven temperature guide

	Electricity °C	Electricity °F	Electricity (fan) °C	Gas Mark
Very cool	110	225	90	$^1/_4$
	120	250	100	$^1/_2$
Cool	140	275	120	1
	150	300	130	2
Moderate	160	325	140	3
	170	350	160	4
Moderately hot	190	375	170	5
	200	400	180	6
Hot	220	425	200	7
	230	450	210	8
Very hot	240	475	220	9

Liquid measurements

Metric	Imperial	Australian	US
25ml	1fl oz		
60ml	2fl oz	$^1/_4$ cup	$^1/_4$ cup
75ml	3fl oz		
100ml	3$^1/_2$fl oz		
120ml	4fl oz	$^1/_2$ cup	$^1/_2$ cup
150ml	5fl oz		
180ml	6fl oz	$^3/_4$ cup	$^3/_4$ cup
200ml	7fl oz		
250ml	9fl oz	1 cup	1 cup
300ml	10$^1/_2$fl oz	1$^1/_4$ cups	1$^1/_4$ cups
350ml	12$^1/_2$fl oz	1$^1/_2$ cups	1$^1/_2$ cups
400ml	14fl oz	1$^3/_4$ cups	1$^3/_4$ cups
450ml	16fl oz	2 cups	2 cups
600ml	1 pint	2$^1/_2$ cups	2$^1/_2$ cups
750ml	1$^1/_4$ pints	3 cups	3 cups
900ml	1$^1/_2$ pints	3$^1/_2$ cups	3$^1/_2$ cups
1 litre	1$^3/_4$ pints	1 quart or 4 cups	1 quart or 4 cups
1.2 litres	2 pints		
1.4 litres	2$^1/_2$ pints		
1.5 litres	2$^3/_4$ pints		
1.7 litres	3 pints		
2 litres	3$^1/_2$ pints		

essential extras

Here's my list of suggested 50–150 calorie foods that you can use to supplement the 123 Plan. All calories listed in this list are approximate; a few wayward calories here and there won't make a difference to your allowance. See page 6 for more information on essential extras and how they fit into the plan. I've also listed some 'free' vegetable ideas, of which you can eat as much as you like! Make sure your plate is half filled with vegetables or salad, or serve them in a large bowl on the side. Eating more greens will help fill you up and provide lots of extra nutrients in your diet. Your skin will look better and the weight should drop off.

50 CALORIES PER SERVING

30g (about 5) ready-to-eat dried apricots
15g (1 tbsp) light mayo
30g (2 tbsp) hummus
40g drained artichoke antipasti in oil
60g whole olives

4 fresh apricots
200g fresh blackberries
200g fresh blackcurrants
100g fresh cherries
2 clementines or satsumas
100g fresh figs
½ grapefruit
85g grapes
2 kiwis
100g fresh mango
200g melon
1 medium nectarine
1 medium orange
1 medium peach
1 medium pear
125g fresh pineapple
100g canned pineapple in juice
2 plums
200g papaya
100g pomegranate seeds
200g raspberries
200g strawberries

100g fresh tomato salsa
50g tzatziki
1 level tbsp orange marmalade
1 level tbsp mango chutney
1 level tsp taramasalata
1 level tbsp honey

2cm slice (about 20g) ciabatta
1 x 10g rye crispbread, such as Ryvita
50g cooked puy lentils, green lentils
1 x measure (25ml) spirits (light or dark, e.g. rum, vodka)

1 tbsp single cream
1 tbsp half-fat crème fraiche
10g Parmesan
30g soft French goat's cheese
25g (1½ tbsp) light soft cheese
150ml orange juice (not from concentrate)
100ml regular soy milk
100g low-fat natural yoghurt
50g (about 3 wafer thin slices) of ham, turkey or chicken

75 CALORIES PER SERVING

150ml semi-skimmed milk
100g low-fat cottage cheese
25g (small wedge) Camembert
1 tbsp double cream
1 tbsp crème fraiche
50g ricotta cheese
¼ 125g ball of fresh mozzarella

¼ average avocado (35g)
50g smoked salmon
1 rasher back bacon, grilled or dry-fried
50g cooked, skinless chicken breast
100g cooked jumbo prawns (about 9)

1 medium apple
100g blueberries
25g dried mango

2 cream crackers
20g rice cakes (2 or 3)
20g plain breadsticks (about 4)
½ English muffin
1 slice medium white or brown bread
15g shop-bought (not takeaway) prawn crackers
1 oatcake

½ 160g tin tuna in brine, drained
40g sun-dried (or sun-blush) tomatoes in oil, drained
30g (2 tbsp) raisins
1 medium egg, boiled

100 CALORIES PER SERVING

1 large egg
40g feta cheese
100g plain cottage cheese
50g (2½ tbsp) soured cream
25g blue cheese
100ml fresh custard
25g cooking chorizo
30g ready-to-eat chorizo
   (about 5 thin slices)
25g salami (about 5 thin
   slices)
1 heaped tbsp pesto

45g Parma ham
   (about 3 slices)
30g smoked mackerel fillet
1 medium banana

1 level tbsp peanut butter
1 tbsp extra virgin olive oil
30g popping corn kernels
20g unsalted plain cashews
20g tortilla chips
25g wasabi peas

20g plain crisps

1 slice of thick cut bread
½ plain bagel
1 x 45g soft white bread roll
½ regular pitta bread
1 slice German style rye bread
1 crumpet
120g baked beans
45g dried couscous
30g dried wholewheat pasta
25g dried soba noodles
30g dried quinoa

125ml wine (white, red, rose)
125ml sparkling wine/
   Champagne
½ pint lager
½ pint bitter
½ pint dry cider

150 CALORIES PER SERVING

35g Cheddar cheese
100g skinless chicken breast,
   baked or grilled

100g cooked brown rice
115g cooked easy-cook white
   rice
40g dried basmati rice
1 potato, baked, boiled or
   mashed without fat
   (195g raw weight)
130g baked sweet potato
   (about ½ large potato)
40g dried rice noodles
50g dried egg noodles
100g cooked pasta
40g porridge oats
50g shop-bought naan bread
   (about ½)

25g unsalted almonds
175ml wine (not sparkling)

'FREE' SAUCES

Brown sauce, in moderation;
   each tbsp is 24 calories
Fish sauce (nam pla)
Ketchup, in moderation;
   each tbsp is 20 calories
Horseradish sauce
Hot sauce (Tabasco)
Mint sauce (not jelly)
Mustard, any variety (English,
   Dijon, wholegrain,
   American)
Soy sauce
Vinegars (balsamic, white
   wine, malt, etc.)
Worcestershire sauce

Any herbs or spices

'FREE' VEGETABLES

Artichokes, including tinned
   hearts (but not in oil)
Asparagus
Aubergine
Baby sweetcorn
Beans, any green (not baked)
   (French, runner, etc.)
Bean sprouts
Beetroot, fresh, cooked
   or pickled
Broccoli
Brussels sprouts
Butternut squash
Cabbage, all kinds
   (Savoy, red, white)
Carrots
Cauliflower
Celeriac
Celery
Chicory
Chillies, including pickled
   jalapeños
Cornichons
Courgettes
Cucumber
Fennel
Garlic
Kale
Leeks
Lemons
Limes
Lettuce and salad greens
   (watercress, baby
   spinach, romaine)
Mangetout
Marrow
Mushrooms
Onions
Peppers
Pickled onions
Radishes
Shallots
Spring onions
Sugar snap peas
Swede
Tomatoes, including tinned
   (but not sun-dried)
Turnips

nutritional information

per serving

page 10 / serves 4
summer minestrone

151 energy (kcal)
636 energy (kJ)
6.6 protein (g)
26.1 carbohydrate (g)
3.0 fat (g)
0.6 saturated fat (g)
8.2 fibre (g)
14.0 sugars (g)

page 12 / serves 4
creamy chicken and parmesan fettucini

374 energy (kcal)
1582 energy (kJ)
32.4 protein (g)
44.6 carbohydrate (g)
8.6 fat (g)
4.4 saturated fat (g)
2.4 fibre (g)
5.4 sugars (g)

page 14 / serves 4
easy green chicken curry with spinach rice

403 energy (kcal)
1691 energy (kJ)
32.9 protein (g)
43.7 carbohydrate (g)
10.5 fat (g)
6.6 saturated fat (g)
3.7 fibre (g)
8.1 sugars (g)

page 16 / serves 3
stir fried orange beef with spring onion rice

369 energy (kcal)
224 energy (kJ)
30.9 protein (g)
37.6 carbohydrate (g)
10.8 fat (g)
3.1 saturated fat (g)
3.7 fibre (g)
10.7 sugars (g)

page 18 / serves 4
italian marsala pork with spinach rice

458 energy (kcal)
1928 energy (kJ)
30.1 protein (g)
54.3 carbohydrate (g)
13.5 fat (g)
2.3 saturated fat (g)
3.0 fibre (g)
5.6 sugars (g)

page 20 / serves 4
spicy sausage pasta

503 energy (kcal)
2112 energy (kJ)
24.9 protein (g)
47.8 carbohydrate (g)
22.2 fat (g)
8.3 saturated fat (g)
3.6 fibre (g)
9.9 sugars (g)

page 22 / serves 4
pea and prosciutto pasta

329 energy (kcal)
1384 energy (kJ)
14.6 protein (g)
42.3 carbohydrate (g)
11.4 fat (g)
5.9 saturated fat (g)
2.9 fibre (g)
2.4 sugars (g)

page 24 / serves 2
broccoli, tuna and lemon chilli spaghetti

315 energy (kcal)
1331 energy (kJ)
23.8 protein (g)
40.1 carbohydrate (g)
7.6 fat (g)
1.2 saturated fat (g)
5.2 fibre (g)
4.5 sugars (g)

page 26 / serves 4
hoisin salmon with spring onion rice

473 energy (kcal)
1991 energy (kJ)
32.4 protein (g)
48.8 carbohydrate (g)
17.8 fat (g)
3.2 saturated fat (g)
0.5 fibre (g)
0.3 sugars (g)

page 28 / serves 2
tagliatelle with smoked salmon

446 energy (kcal)
1876 energy (kJ)
19.1 protein (g)
52.7 carbohydrate (g)
17.4 fat (g)
9.5 saturated fat (g)
3.6 fibre (g)
3.6 sugars (g)

page 30 / serves 2
spaghetti omelette

406 energy (kcal)
1694 energy (kJ)
24.0 protein (g)
19.9 carbohydrate (g)
26.2 fat (g)
10.0 saturated fat (g)
2.8 fibre (g)
3.6 sugars (g)

page 34 / serves 4
creamy chicken and vegetable pasta

310 energy (kcal)
1310 energy (kJ)
26.5 protein (g)
34.6 carbohydrate (g)
7.4 fat (g)
2.9 saturated fat (g)
2.2 fibre (g)
2.1 sugars (g)

page 36 / serves 4
**chicken tikka and
saffron rice**

343/24* energy (kcal)
1444/101* energy (kJ)
40.7/2.3* protein (g)
35.6/3.6* carb (g)
4.3/0.1* fat (g)
0.7/0* saturated fat (g)
3.0/0.2* fibre (g)
8.5/3.3* sugars (g)
*minted yoghurt

page 38 / serves 6
spaghetti bolognese

367 energy (kcal)
1551 energy (kJ)
28.5 protein (g)
41.7 carbohydrate (g)
9.3 fat (g)
3.7 saturated fat (g)
5.5 fibre (g)
8.2 sugars (g)

page 40 / serves 6
**home-made meatballs
with tagliatelle**

384 energy (kcal)
1613 energy (kJ)
26.1 protein (g)
40.7 carbohydrate (g)
12.3 fat (g)
4.4 saturated fat (g)
4.9 fibre (g)
7.9 sugars (g)

page 42 / serves 5
**frying pan beef
lasagne**

444 energy (kcal)
1858 energy (kJ)
36.6 protein (g)
25.7 carbohydrate (g)
19.8 fat (g)
10.2 saturated fat (g)
4.5 fibre (g)
9.3 sugars (g)

page 44 / serves 2
**simple tagliatelle
carbonara**

416 energy (kcal)
1744 energy (kJ)
18.4 protein (g)
41.0 carbohydrate (g)
21.0 fat (g)
11.7 saturated fat (g)
5.0 fibre (g)
3.8 sugars (g)

page 46 / serves 4
sausage pasta pot

373 energy (kcal)
1568 energy (kJ)
18.8 protein (g)
47.0 carbohydrate (g)
12.7 fat (g)
3.5 saturated fat (g)
5.1 fibre (g)
11.5 sugars (g)

page 48 / serves 4
pasta puttanesca

261 energy (kcal)
1103 energy (kJ)
9.5 protein (g)
42.3 carbohydrate (g)
7.2 fat (g)
1.0 saturated fat (g)
4.5 fibre (g)
6.0 sugars (g)

page 50 / serves 4
**cauliflower macaroni
cheese**

317 energy (kcal)
1333 energy (kJ)
13.5 protein (g)
39.7 carbohydrate (g)
12.7 fat (g)
7.4 saturated fat (g)
3.8 fibre (g)
7.0 sugars (g)

page 52 / serves 6
veggie bolognese

314 energy (kcal)
1331 energy (kJ)
16.1 protein (g)
56.5 carbohydrate (g)
4.0 fat (g)
0.5 saturated fat (g)
8.9 fibre (g)
10.4 sugars (g)

page 54 / serves 5
**roast vegetable, goat's
cheese and sun-dried
tomato pasta**

310 energy (kcal)
1308 energy (kJ)
9.8 protein (g)
50.9 carbohydrate (g)
8.0 fat (g)
2.1 saturated fat (g)
4.6 fibre (g)
10.0 sugars (g)

page 56 / serves 4
**blue cheese and
spinach rigatoni**

340 energy (kcal)
1428 energy (kJ)
14.1 protein (g)
43.3 carbohydrate (g)
12.5 fat (g)
7.1 saturated fat (g)
2.6 fibre (g)
5.8 sugars (g)

page 60 / serves 4
**chicken, mushroom
and pea risotto**

354 energy (kcal)
1494 energy (kJ)
34.5 protein (g)
35.4 carbohydrate (g)
6.7 fat (g)
2.1 saturated fat (g)
3.2 fibre (g)
3.1 sugars (g)

page 62 / serves 4
hunter's risotto

448 energy (kcal)
1887 energy (kJ)
36.6 protein (g)
46.7 carbohydrate (g)
9.9 fat (g)
3.0 saturated fat (g)
3.0 fibre (g)
6.0 sugars (g)

page 64 / serves 6
persian lamb pilaf

458 energy (kcal)
1916 energy (kJ)
33.1 protein (g)
42.8 carbohydrate (g)
17.4 fat (g)
5.5 saturated fat (g)
2.6 fibre (g)
14.1 sugars (g)

page 66 / serves 4
ham and leek risotto

319 energy (kcal)
1341 energy (kJ)
12.6 protein (g)
43.4 carbohydrate (g)
8.8 fat (g)
3.5 saturated fat (g)
2.8 fibre (g)
3.0 sugars (g)

page 68 / serves 2
asparagus and lemon risotto

304 energy (kcal)
1280 energy (kJ)
10.5 protein (g)
44.8 carbohydrate (g)
7.6 fat (g)
2.9 saturated fat (g)
2.5 fibre (g)
4.1 sugars (g)

page 70 / serves 5
roast squash, spinach and sage risotto

329 energy (kcal)
1388 energy (kJ)
9.5 protein (g)
49.8 carbohydrate (g)
8.3 fat (g)
2.6 saturated fat (g)
5.1 fibre (g)
10.9 sugars (g)

page 72 / makes 14
oven-baked arancini

79 energy (kcal)
335 energy (kJ)
2.8 protein (g)
14.9 carbohydrate (g)
1.0 fat (g)
0.2 saturated fat (g)
0.9 fibre (g)
0.6 sugars (g)

page 74 / serves 4
skinny kedgeree

358 energy (kcal)
1506 energy (kJ)
24.7 protein (g)
38.3 carbohydrate (g)
12.8 fat (g)
4.8 saturated fat (g)
2.3 fibre (g)
5.1 sugars (g)

page 76 / serves 4
pilau rice

178 energy (kcal)
745 energy (kJ)
3.5 protein (g)
36.6 carbohydrate (g)
1.8 fat (g)
0.2 saturated fat (g)
0.4 fibre (g)
1.1 sugars (g)

page 78 / serves 5
mushroom rice

205 energy (kcal)
853 energy (kJ)
4.3 protein (g)
34.7 carbohydrate (g)
5.2 fat (g)
2.7 saturated fat (g)
1.3 fibre (g)
1.9 sugars (g)

page 82 / serves 5
roast chicken and savoury rice

517/71* energy (kcal)
2180/295* energy (kJ)
46.9/0.1* protein (g)
49.8/2.7* carbohydrate (g)
15.8/6.7* fat (g)
4.0/0.9* saturated fat (g)
2.5/0.1* fibre (g)
5.9/2.4* sugars (g)
*balsamic vinaigrette

page 84 / serves 6
moroccan chicken tagine

391 energy (kcal)
1649 energy (kJ)
39.5 protein (g)
42.0 carbohydrate (g)
8.3 fat (g)
1.7 saturated fat (g)
7.5 fibre (g)
14.5 sugars (g)

page 86 / serves 6
slow cooked beef ragu

306/190* energy (kcal)
1284/804* energy (kJ)
29.6/6.0* protein (g)
8.8/37.1* carb (g)
13.6/3.0* fat (g)
5.3/1.4* sat fat (g)
2.3/1.9* fibre (g)
7.4/1.7* sugars (g)
*buttered tagliatelle

page 88 / serves 6
spaghetti pie

354 energy (kcal)
1491 energy (kJ)
27.8 protein (g)
33.1 carbohydrate (g)
12.0 fat (g)
5.7 saturated fat (g)
3.7 fibre (g)
9.2 sugars (g)

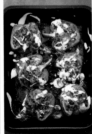

page 90 / serves 6
hungarian turkey stuffed peppers

186 energy (kcal)
779 energy (kJ)
13.1 protein (g)
20.0 carbohydrate (g)
6.4 fat (g)
2.6 saturated fat (g)
3.0 fibre (g)
8.2 sugars (g)

page 92 / serves 6
tuscan pork ragu

508 energy (kcal)
2136 energy (kJ)
33.0 protein (g)
49.0 carbohydrate (g)
17.6 fat (g)
4.8 saturated fat (g)
5.3 fibre (g)
11.3 sugars (g)

page 94 / makes 6
baked tomatoes with spiced lamb

191 energy (kcal)
805 energy (kJ)
11.5 protein (g)
21.1 carbohydrate (g)
6.9 fat (g)
2.7 saturated fat (g)
4.2 fibre (g)
11.0 sugars (g)

page 96 / serves 4
chinese-style sea bass

322 energy (kcal)
1353 energy (kJ)
28.3 protein (g)
32.2 carbohydrate (g)
9.2 fat (g)
1.5 saturated fat (g)
3.8 fibre (g)
13.0 sugars (g)

page 98 / serves 4
ricotta and spinach pasta parcels

400 energy (kcal)
1665 energy (kJ)
19.1 protein (g)
40.0 carbohydrate (g)
17.1 fat (g)
7.3 saturated fat (g)
6.5 fibre (g)
9.0 sugars (g)

page 102 / serves 4
chicken pho

314 energy (kcal)
1315 energy (kJ)
29.6 protein (g)
30.9 carbohydrate (g)
7.5 fat (g)
2.0 saturated fat (g)
2.6 fibre (g)
2.6 sugars (g)

page 104 / serves 4
**royal chicken korma
with coriander rice**

499 energy (kcal)
2091 energy (kJ)
43.3 protein (g)
50.6 carbohydrate (g)
13.7 fat (g)
4.8 saturated fat (g)
1.4 fibre (g)
8.8 sugars (g)

page 106 / serves 6
**jerk chicken with rice
and beans**

466 energy (kcal)
1969 energy (kJ)
42.3 protein (g)
50.6 carb (g)
12.0 fat (g)
6.3 saturated fat (g)
5.4 fibre (g)
8.7 sugars (g)

page 108 / serves 4
pad thai

377 energy (kcal)
1577 energy (kJ)
27.8 protein (g)
39.4 carbohydrate (g)
11.8 fat (g)
2.4 saturated fat (g)
2.1 fibre (g)
6.6 sugars (g)

page 110 / makes 8
hoisin pork rolls

126 energy (kcal)
531 energy (kJ)
7.3 protein (g)
16.1 carbohydrate (g)
3.8 fat (g)
1.2 saturated fat (g)
0.9 fibre (g)
2.0 sugars (g)

page 112 / serves 4
singapore noodles

302 energy (kcal)
1271 energy (kJ)
29.3 protein (g)
31.6 carbohydrate (g)
7.1 fat (g)
1.6 saturated fat (g)
3.0 fibre (g)
5.5 sugars (g)

page 114 / makes 12
crab sushi rolls

69 energy (kcal)
294 energy (kJ)
3.2 protein (g)
12.7 carbohydrate (g)
0.6 fat (g)
0.1 saturated fat (g)
2.6 fibre (g)
1.1 sugars (g)

page 116 / makes 12
**salmon and avocado
nigiri sushi**

53 energy (kcal)
223 energy (kJ)
1.8 protein (g)
8.1 carbohydrate (g)
1.4 fat (g)
0.3 saturated fat (g)
1.7 fibre (g)
0.7 sugars (g)

page 118 / makes 12
**salmon, rice and
coriander cakes**

64/65* energy (kcal)
270/275* energy (kJ)
4.1/0.7* protein (g)
6.7/15.4* carbohydrate (g)
2.3/0.2* fat (g)
0.4/0.1* saturated fat (g)
0.1/0.9* fibre (g)
0.2/15.1* sugars (g)
*tomato and chilli jam

page 120 / serves 6
simple spanish paella

400 energy (kcal)
1691 energy (kJ)
39.6 protein (g)
40.3 carbohydrate (g)
9.1 fat (g)
2.5 saturated fat (g)
2.5 fibre (g)
5.2 sugars (g)

page 122 / serves 2
**linguine with scallops
and prawns**

490 energy (kcal)
2068 energy (kJ)
33.5 protein (g)
58.4 carbohydrate (g)
13.4 fat (g)
2.1 saturated fat (g)
3.9 fibre (g)
3.4 sugars (g)

page 126 / serves 4
**sesame chicken
noodle salad**

330 energy (kcal)
1389 energy (kJ)
35.7 protein (g)
35.2 carbohydrate (g)
5.7 fat (g)
1.1 saturated fat (g)
5.4 fibre (g)
15.5 sugars (g)

page 128 / serves 3
**spiced chicken and
rice salad**

418 energy (kcal)
1761 energy (kJ)
34.4 protein (g)
45.2 carbohydrate (g)
12.3 fat (g)
1.7 saturated fat (g)
3.6 fibre (g)
15.0 sugars (g)

page 130 / serves 4
**barbecue-style
chicken pasta salad**

399 energy (kcal)
1686 energy (kJ)
33.9 protein (g)
47.7 carbohydrate (g)
8.6 fat (g)
1.7 saturated fat (g)
3.0 fibre (g)
13.1 sugars (g)

page 132 / serves 4
**pesto chicken pasta
salad**

431 energy (kcal)
1809 energy (kJ)
21.0 protein (g)
39.7 carbohydrate (g)
20.9 fat (g)
3.2 saturated fat (g)
1.0 fibre (g)
2.6 sugars (g)

page 134 / serves 4
prawn and pasta layer salad

205 energy (kcal)
863 energy (kJ)
15.9 protein (g)
23.1 carbohydrate (g)
5.8 fat (g)
0.8 saturated fat (g)
2.2 fibre (g)
6.9 sugars (g)

page 136 / serves 2
lime and coriander salmon salad

332 energy (kcal)
1388 energy (kJ)
21.9 protein (g)
26.0 carbohydrate (g)
15.7 fat (g)
2.4 saturated fat (g)
3.2 fibre (g)
5.8 sugars (g)

page 138 / serves 2
prawn noodle salad

223 energy (kcal)
936 energy (kJ)
20.3 protein (g)
32.9 carbohydrate (g)
1.3 fat (g)
0.3 saturated fat (g)
3.8 fibre (g)
15.0 sugars (g)

page 140 / serves 4
tomato, basil and mozzarella pasta salad

333 energy (kcal)
1400 energy (kJ)
13.9 protein (g)
41.9 carbohydrate (g)
12.2 fat (g)
5.3 saturated fat (g)
1.9 fibre (g)
4.3 sugars (g)

page 142 / serves 4
mediterranean vegetable and giant couscous salad

159 energy (kcal)
660 energy (kJ)
5.3 protein (g)
26.2 carbohydrate (g)
4.1 fat (g)
0.6 saturated fat (g)
5.0 fibre (g)
7.7 sugars (g)

page 146 / serves 2
fresh tomato sauce

133 energy (kcal)
554 energy (kJ)
1.3 protein (g)
6.5 carbohydrate (g)
11.6 fat (g)
1.8 saturated fat (g)
2.1 fibre (g)
5.7 sugars (g)

page 148 / serves 4
magic cauliflower sauce

126 energy (kcal)
528 energy (kJ)
5.2 protein (g)
10.1 carbohydrate (g)
7.5 fat (g)
4.5 saturated fat (g)
1.6 fibre (g)
5.1 sugars (g)

page 150 / serves 4
simple tomato pasta sauce

96 energy (kcal)
404 energy (kJ)
3.0 protein (g)
15.0 carbohydrate (g)
3.1 fat (g)
0.4 saturated fat (g)
3.3 fibre (g)
12.7 sugars (g)

page 152 / serves 4
creamy tomato and chilli pasta sauce

130 energy (kcal)
544 energy (kJ)
3.0 protein (g)
9.8 carbohydrate (g)
9.1 fat (g)
4.2 saturated fat (g)
2.6 fibre (g)
8.1 sugars (g)

page 154 / serves 4
mushroom sauce for pasta

102 energy (kcal)
427 energy (kJ)
3.3 protein (g)
8.0 carbohydrate (g)
5.6 fat (g)
2.6 saturated fat (g)
1.2 fibre (g)
2.5 sugars (g)

page 156 / serves 6
broccoli pesto

91 energy (kcal)
376 energy (kJ)
3.5 protein (g)
1.1 carbohydrate (g)
8.1 fat (g)
1.3 saturated fat (g)
1.0 fibre (g)
0.6 sugars (g)

page 158 / serves 4
sweet roasted tomatoes and thyme

53 energy (kcal)
220 energy (kJ)
1.1 protein (g)
4.3 carbohydrate (g)
3.6 fat (g)
0.6 saturated fat (g)
1.7 fibre (g)
3.9 sugars (g)

page 162 / serves 6
**lemon rice puddings
with raspberries**

146 energy (kcal)
620 energy (kJ)
5.2 protein (g)
26.9 carbohydrate (g)
2.3 fat (g)
1.3 saturated fat (g)
1.1 fibre (g)
8.9 sugars (g)

page 164 / serves 5
**spiced apple rice
pudding**

209 energy (kcal)
888 energy (kJ)
6.2 protein (g)
42.3 carbohydrate (g)
2.3 fat (g)
1.3 saturated fat (g)
2.0 fibre (g)
22.7 sugars (g)

page 166 / makes 16
shortbread fingers

154 energy (kcal)
642 energy (kJ)
1.6 protein (g)
19.7 carbohydrate (g)
2.9 fat (g)
4.9 saturated fat (g)
0.7 fibre (g)
5.2 sugars (g)

page 168 / serves 6
**roasted figs with rose
rice**

172 energy (kcal)
728 energy (kJ)
6.2 protein (g)
25.8 carbohydrate (g)
5.4 fat (g)
2.4 saturated fat (g)
1.3 fibre (g)
17.1 sugars (g)

page 170 / serves 6
apple noodle kugel

179 energy (kcal)
759 energy (kJ)
3.6 protein (g)
37.4 carbohydrate (g)
2.7 fat (g)
1.4 saturated fat (g)
3.5 fibre (g)
19.7 sugars (g)

page 172 / makes 9
florentine rice cakes

64 energy (kcal)
267 energy (kJ)
1.2 protein (g)
7.7 carbohydrate (g)
3.0 fat (g)
1.1 saturated fat (g)
0.3 fibre (g)
3.5 sugars (g)

page 174 / serves 6
chocolate risotto cups

162 energy (kcal)
685 energy (kJ)
5.3 protein (g)
23.6 carbohydrate (g)
5.2 fat (g)
3.0 saturated fat (g)
0.1 fibre (g)
6.7 sugars (g)

index

First published in Great Britain in 2016
by Orion Publishing Group Ltd
Carmelite House
50 Victoria Embankment
London, EC4Y 0DZ
An Hachette UK Company

10 9 8 7 6 5 4 3 2

Text © Justine Pattison 2016
Design and layout © Orion 2016

A CIP catalogue record for this book is available
from the British Library.
ISBN: 978 1 4091 5475 4

Designer: Smith & Gilmour
Photographer: Cristian Barnett
Props stylist: Claire Bignell
Creative director: Justine Pattison
Nutritional analysis calculated by: Lauren Brignell
Recipe assistants: Rebecca Roberts, Annabel Wray,
Charlotte Page
Kitchen assistants: Jess Blain, Emily PB, Hasmita Gohil
Project editor: Jillian Young
Copy editor: Elise See Tai
Proofreader: Mary-Jane Wilkins
Indexer: Rosemary Dear

Printed and bound in Italy

*Every effort has been made to ensure that the
information in this book is accurate. The information
will be relevant to the majority of people but may not
be applicable in each individual case, so it is advised
that professional medical advice is obtained for
specific health matters. Neither the publisher nor
author accept any legal responsibility for any personal
injury or other damage or loss arising from the use or
misuse of the information in this book. Anyone making
a change in their diet should consult their GP,
especially if pregnant, infirm, elderly or under 16.*

Acknowledgements

Firstly, huge thanks to everyone who enjoys my recipes
and the way I cook. You have given me such fantastic
feedback; I hope you like these dishes just as much.

An enormous thank you to my family; John, Jess and
Emily, for greeting each new recipe enthusiastically,
even when you'd been given pasta for supper 12 days
in a row.

I'm truly grateful to the very talented photographer
Cristian Barnett for wonderful photographs that really
make my food come to life. And the brilliant Claire
Bignell for her superb creative skills, selecting the
perfect props and helping make the recipes look
both beautiful and achievable. Massive thanks to
Lauren Brignell for all her invaluable nutritional
support and the hundreds of recipes she has analysed
over the past few months. Also, thanks to Rebecca
Roberts for testing the recipes and assisting on shoot
days. Not forgetting Annabel Wray, Annie Simpson
and Charlotte Page for their hard work in the test
kitchen.

At Orion, I would like to thank Amanda Harris for
believing in this project right from the beginning and
for trusting me to get on and develop the series. Also
thank you to Jillian Young, my fantastic editor, for her
guidance and professionalism, Lucy Haenlein for
taking in my last minute tweaks so patiently and Helen
Ewing for her design support.

A big thank you to everyone at Smith & Gilmour for
making the books look eye-catching, practical and
readable. I'm also grateful to my agent, Zoe King, at
The Blair Partnership, for her constant encouragement
and enthusiasm.

And a final thank you to the rest of my family and my
friends for their fantastic support.